iCT for Learners with Special Needs

ICT for Learners with Special Needs

A handbook for tutors

**Nicole Taylor and
John Chacksfield**

David Fulton Publishers

David Fulton Publishers Ltd
The Chiswick Centre, 414 Chiswick High Road, London W4 5TF

www.fultonpublishers.co.uk

David Fulton Publishers is a division of Granada Learning Ltd, part of ITV plc.

British Library Cataloguing in Publication Data
A catalogue record for this book is available from the British Library.

ISBN 1-84312-325-8

10 9 8 7 6 5 4 3 2 1

Designed and typeset by Kenneth Burnley, Wirral, Cheshire
Printed and bound in Great Britain

ICT for Learners with Special Needs

A handbook for tutors

Nicole Taylor and
John Chacksfield

Royal College of
Occupational
Therapists

WITHDRAWN

 David Fulton Publishers

David Fulton Publishers Ltd
The Chiswick Centre, 414 Chiswick High Road, London W4 5TF

www.fultonpublishers.co.uk

David Fulton Publishers is a division of Granada Learning Ltd, part of ITV plc.

British Library Cataloguing in Publication Data
A catalogue record for this book is available from the British Library.

ISBN 1-84312-325-8

10 9 8 7 6 5 4 3 2 1

Designed and typeset by Kenneth Burnley, Wirral, Cheshire
Printed and bound in Great Britain

Contents

Contents of the CD-ROM

Large icon cards

Alignment icon
Bold, Italic and Underline icon
Font Colour icon
Font Size icon
Font Style icon
Large icons sheet
New Page icon
Save icon

Group 1

Scheme of work for Group 1
Session plans for Group 1
Tutor notes for Group 1
Session 1 resources
Building the computer exercise
How to turn on the computer handout
Mouse control skills 1
Mouse control skills 2
Mouse control skills questions
The computer system disk exercise
Session 2 resources
Computer components matching exercise
Changing the size practice
Changing the colour practice
Session 3 resources
Icons exercise
Matching jobs and places
Jobs word completion
Jobs typing skills
Jobs picture search
Session 4 resources
Matching objects and activities
Objects and activities word completion
Objects and activities typing skills
Objects and activities picture search
Session 5 resources
Matching people, animal and homes
People, animals and homes word completion
People, animals and homes typing skills
People, animals and homes picture search
Session 6 resources
Matching transport
Transport word completion
Transport typing skills
Transport picture search
Session 7 resources
Matching holidays and equipment
Holiday word completion
Holiday typing skills
Holiday picture search
Holiday word search

Session 8 resources
Matching signs
Signs word completion
Signs typing skills
Signs picture search
Signs word search
Session 9 resources
Matching families exercise
Families word completion
Family typing skills
Backgrounds and family figures
Session 10 resources
Matching countries and landmarks exercise
Countries and landmarks word completion
Countries and landmarks typing skills
Miniature landmarks, flags and map
Session 11 resources
Matching food and shops exercise
Food word completion
Food typing skills
Healthy foods exercise
Session 12 resources
Seasonal things to do
Seasons exercise

Group 2

Scheme of work for Group 2
Session plans for Group 2
Tutor notes for Group 2
Session 1 resources
Computer components handout
How to turn on the computer
How to log on to MS Word
The MS Word screen
Windows basics exercise
Computer components picture cards
Blank MS Word screen
Word processing checklist
How to highlight text
Change the size and style
BIU disk work
Session 2 resources
Components recap
Word basics
Icons handout
Inserting 1 disk work
Inserting 1 worksheet
Deleting 1 disk work
Deleting 1 worksheet
Saving a document
Opening a document
About me
About my lesson
Session 2 worksheet

Session 3 resources
Inserting 2
Deleting 2
Alignments example sheet
Alignment practice disk work
Colour and alignment practice disk work
Matching the icons 1
Adverts example sheet
Flyer example
Invitation example
Session 4 resources
Basic formatting worksheet
How to copy and paste handout
How to cut and paste handout
Copy and paste practice
Cut and paste practice
Computer skills crossword
Line Spacing example
How to change the Line Spacing handout
Line Spacing disk work
Session 4 worksheet
Session 5 resources
Session 5 recap
Spellcheck 1
Spellcheck 2
How to change the margins
Page Setup recap
How to use Find and Replace
Find and Replace practice
What goes where
Practice exercise
Session 6 resources
Recap exercise 1
Recap exercise 2
Recap exercise 3
Recap exercise 4
Session 7 resources
How to insert ClipArt
How to move pictures
How to resize pictures
How to crop pictures
How to insert a picture saved on disk
Disk work with pictures
Inserting graphics exercise
Session 8 resources
How to add WordArt
Matching the icons 2
How to add page borders 1
How to add page borders 2
Graphics worksheet 1
Graphics worksheet 2
Session 9 resources
How to add AutoShapes
How to add colour to AutoShapes
How to change AutoShape lines
AutoShape picture 1
AutoShape picture 2
Graphics quiz

Session 10 resources
Letter format
Practice letter
Letter exercise disk work
Miss Jones letter
How to insert a symbol
Inserting symbols exercise
How to add a bulleted_numbered list
Bullets and numbering disk work
Session 10 worksheet
Session 11 resources
What's wrong with this letter
Creating tables
Word search
Merging cells
Session 12 resources
Recap skills quiz

Group 3

Scheme of work for Group 3
Session plans for Group 3
Tutor notes for Group 3
Session 1 resources
Computer components handout
How to turn on the computer
Mouse control skills 1
Mouse control skills 2
Session 2 resources
Components recap
Computer components jigsaw
How to turn on the computer
Session 3 resources
How to log on to the internet
Internet Explorer web browser
Web addresses
Using links exercise
Internet basics quiz
Session 4 resources
How to search for information
Quiz
Session 5 resources
Travel signs
Travel pictures exercise
Holiday word search
Session 7 resources
My Home passage
Home hazards worksheet
Session 8 resources
My Area passage
Hazards outside worksheet
Session 9 resources
My Activities passage
Activity hazards worksheet
Session 10 resources
My Job passage
Job hazards worksheet
Session 11 resources
Feedback form
Form 2

About the authors

Nicole Taylor

Nicole Taylor is an adult education tutor who specialises in teaching ICT to adults with mental health needs, learning disabilities and adults in the mainstream. In addition, she has worked with culture- and gender-specific groups, such as Jewish women, Muslim women, Asian women, refugees and their children.

Nicole has worked for London Borough of Tower Hamlets Lifelong Learning, Hackney Community College, East London and the City Mental Health NHS Trust and Living Space (a mental health charity). She is also a Director for Southside Rehabilitation Association, a registered charity for helping people with a mental illness return to meaningful employment.

One of Nicole's particular achievements has been setting up the ICT resource in a mental health day hospital in East London and facilitating one of the first ever ECDL training programmes for adults with special needs in a UK mental health trust.

John Chacksfield

John is an occupational therapist and manager in the NHS. He has worked with younger adults (aged 18–65) in a wide range of mental health settings, including general mental health, forensic mental health, substance misuse and learning disabilities. Recently he managed a community service for adults with a dual diagnosis of mental health and substance misuse within South London and and is now Head of Therapies within East London and the City Mental Health NHS Trust (City and Hackney Locality).

John has a postgraduate certificate in education and has taught various professionals about working with people with disabilities. He has also written several book chapters and academic papers for occupational therapists and other professionals working in mental health.

Foreword

Special skills and insights into helping people with special needs

At a *worldwide* level, political leaders have recognised that the 'rich' countries are rich in information and communication resources and that, if the 'poor' countries are ever to overcome severe inequalities, they must develop their capacities in ICT. Only recently have people in affluent societies such Britain and the USA realised, *within* each community, that adults with disabilities not only need to develop ICT skills to participate fully in their own society, but that achieving confidence in ICT reduces many disabilities.

Education has led the way in England with the Special Educational Needs and Disability Act 2001. For example, for teachers in both the further education sector and in universities, learners with any special needs should be able to participate fully in the educational opportunities of each institution. Often this involves learner-centred support and equipment, and new insights into the learning experience on the part of their teacher. Thanks to a grant from the Nuffield Foundation, I have observed that even students with multiple disabilities are enabled to complete their courses and to take part in 'student life'. However, the USA is far ahead of the UK in promoting employment for people with special needs. Here, even gaining a university degree does not ensure paid work for adults with disabilities. People with learning disabilities or attention problems following traumatic brain injury are especially likely to become excluded from employment forever. In 2004, the Department for Work and Pensions produced a promising framework for vocational rehabilitation. Not only does this require health services to support people with, say, long-term mental illness in getting and holding down a job, it recognises that participation in paid work is usually good for the long-term health of disabled people.

Taylor and Chacksfield's pioneering book not only has a place in services providing education or rehabilitation, it will bring benefits to many community services aiming at social inclusion. A few years ago, when I was working in some of the poorest boroughs of London, urban regeneration money was funding new 'learning villages' based on ICT to improve the life chances of local residents. However, people with disabilities were not using these new facilities and the council managers were unaware of the potential for ICT in overcoming loneliness and poverty in that disabled population. Thankfully, the situation is now changing in a whole spectrum of community developments, and residents with special needs are now able to participate in the growth of their own 'neighbourhoods'.

This book will help unlock the doors to a great many facilities. I look forward to the day when an adult with special needs has been enabled, say, to run the BBC or the National Health Service.

WOODY CAAN

Professor of Public Health
Anglia Polytechnic University, Chelmsford, Essex

Foreword

This book fills a gap for information and communication technology (ICT) teachers and trainers working with adults. Although the focus of the work is on teaching those learners with special needs, the underpinning philosophy and the practical approaches are relevant to all learners.

ICT skills are essential skills for everyone in society. This is the authors' starting point. Not only are such skills in themselves now recognised as one of the basic skills along with literacy and numeracy, they are also the skills that can support much other learning. This makes the work of those teaching and training in this curriculum area of great importance. These teachers provide access to these skills for a range of learners with special needs. Without ICT skills, people who might already feel like 'outsiders' can have that sense of alienation and isolation increasingly deepened as such skills are more and more widely required.

The authors of this work are committed to an inclusive approach and this book is born of a wish to ensure that as many adults as possible can acquire an understanding of information technology and be able to make use of these skills in their daily lives, for employment, and for further learning.

Teachers and trainers will find the schemes of work, lesson plans and resources very helpful in their day-to-day practice. The accompanying disk will allow all teachers of ICT, whatever the needs of their learners may be, to adapt and customise the material to suit the groups and individuals that they are working with.

The theory behind the approach is clearly presented and reminds practitioners that all learners have individual needs and their own difficulties with learning. Successful teaching and learning depends on those managing the teaching to understand and plan for a wide range of differentiation amongst any group of learners.

MAGGIE FLETCHER

Head of Lifelong Learning
London Borough of Tower Hamlets

Acknowledgements

The authors would particularly like to thank the following who have enabled the book to be completed:

London Borough of Tower Hamlets Lifelong Learning

Granada Learning Ltd

Microsoft Corporation

Texthelp Ltd

Preface

There is a considerable drive across Europe and in the USA, Canada, Australia and other countries to ensure that adults with special needs, such as those with learning disabilities or mental health problems and the elderly, are integrated into society. Information and communication technology (ICT) is becoming central to the world of employment, leisure, social interaction and self-maintenance.

Examples from the UK, such as the white paper for people with learning disabilities, *Valuing People* (Department of Health 2001), emphasise the need for integration of this group of people into all areas of society. The British government's recent Social Exclusion Unit report (Office of the Deputy Prime Minister 2004) reinforces a similar message for people with mental health conditions and highlights the need to improve access to education and employment. The Special Educational Needs and Disability Act 2001 (Department for Education and Skills 2001) places new duties on the bodies responsible for providing post-16 education and related services. These duties are:

- not to treat disabled people and students less favourably, without justification, than students without a disability
- to take reasonable steps to enable disabled people and students to have full access to further and higher education.

ICT is now an enormous part of everyday life. It is becoming vital that people from every sector of the community, including those with various disabilities and the consequent special needs, know how to make use of modern ICT and have the confidence to do so.

Many adults, including those with special needs, now gain the skills to use ICT from within the further education sector. This will become increasingly so with growing government expectations that colleges of further education and adult education services provide appropriate training. College-run training, including classes taught by college tutors but within hospital settings or outreach, is part of a growing and necessary partnership between the health and further education sectors.

This book provides a manual for tutors who need to adapt their teaching to the requirements of adults with special needs, so that these individuals can learn about ICT as successfully as adults in mainstream educational and rehabilitation settings.

Resources and information about specialist equipment and techniques are not easy to come by for many ICT tutors in the adult education sector. Many tutors and trainers have to find out by trial and error on the job. Training courses based around adult special needs are few and far between. Some specialist information is available in the health sector but very little relates to the needs of adults who use mental health services – the only publication is by Wertheimer (1997). Almost all the manuals about special needs are aimed at children and at schools. The only ones for adults appear to focus on literacy and numeracy skills, which, while being important, do not always cover the general principles of work with adult learners with a variety of special needs.

A good example of a text within this area that does address a range of special needs is *Introducing Access for All* (DFES 2003). Although also focused on literacy and numeracy, it is probably the only mainstream document that covers seven key adult special need areas, including people who have mental health problems.

This book, with its focus on ICT, aims to fill a large 'gap in the market'. Adults with special needs are frequently and increasingly engaged in learning about and building confidence with ICT.

The book provides a resource that is easy for trainers to pick up and use in any learning environment, that will help them with session planning and offer ideas for training, and that will ultimately benefit the most important people in the process – the learners themselves.

NICOLE TAYLOR and JOHN CHACKSFIELD

Section 1

Introduction

If you are like us, you probably hate reading introductions – you want to get to the main part of the book. Therefore, we have kept this introduction short and have only included the essential information to show where we are coming from in relation to our ideas.

Who is the book for?

This book has been developed for use by professionals working with adults who have special needs. These professionals are likely to include teachers from the adult education or further education sectors, trainers, occupational therapists, technical instructors and others from the health sector. For simplicity, we have mainly used the term 'trainer' in the book, but please substitute your own title as you read if this is easier.

For anyone beginning their career, the book will be valuable because it provides them with instant lesson plans and easy-to-use resources. For professionals in training, there is a theory base, with clear explanations.

For all professionals, we hope the book will really make things easy: just take whatever resources you need from the accompanying disk. If you are a tutor and a college requires you to produce session plans, you should be able to simply cut and paste ours or just print them off and send them in. We want to make your life as easy as possible.

Please send us any feedback so that future editions of the book will be better and more useful. This can be done via the publisher and their website, www.fultonpublishers.co.uk.

So what are 'special needs'?

'Special needs' is a concept that means different things to different people, depending on your professional background and the accepted language in your particular part of the world. If you are from a teaching background, you may be more familiar with the phrase 'special educational needs', which is often abbreviated to SEN. If you are from a health background, you may be more used to 'disability' or 'mental health needs'. We have chosen 'special needs' to encompass all of these ideas but with a focus on the cognitive aspects of disability.

For the purposes of this book, 'special needs' will refer to:

> The needs which people have that inhibit or prevent them from learning, understanding and solving problems because of cognitive factors or other psychological issues.

The commonly accepted disabilities and health issues that either cause or are linked with various special needs can be categorised as follows:

- learning disabilities (called intellectual disabilities or 'mental retardation' and sometimes 'developmental disability' in the USA and other countries, and formerly called 'mental handicap' in the UK), such as Down's syndrome

- brain damage, caused by physical damage, chemical damage, drug misuse or brain degeneration
- cognitive interruption of learning performance caused by the symptoms of mental illnesses, such as schizophrenia, bipolar disorder, post-traumatic stress disorder or severe depression.

A common feature of these three categories is that they relate to a *developmental frame of reference*, where a person's cognitive capacity has either not developed fully or where this has been reduced or impaired, permanently or temporarily, by damage or illness. Knowing about the developmental aspect of learning can help tailor session planning to the learner. More will be written on this issue later, in Chapter 1.

These conditions will be explored in relation to adults aged 16 or over. Although many of the concepts in this book will be applicable to children and adolescents, many already available texts directly relate to the very specific needs of this group and formal diagnoses.

What the book does not cover

This book does not directly address the needs of people with dyslexia, or other similar conditions that affect the ability to process language, because there are very specific issues faced by these groups. It is recognised that some people with other cognitive disabilities will sometimes have a concurrent dyslexia or similar issue and the reader is referred to books specifically on that subject.

The book does not deal with anyone with a (non-cognitive) physical disability either, as separate information is generally available for this group on adaptation of ICT equipment for their use.

Some groups of older adults (i.e. over 70) do have specific needs related to age or age-related cognitive disability, such as the needs arising from the ageing process as well as from disorders such as dementia, but these issues are best dealt with in their own right in a separate text.

It is likely, however, that some of the exercises in this book will be equally applicable to these groups, and we would leave that decision up to the trainer or user of this manual.

What the book contains

Our primary aim is to present a book that is practical in the way it shows that, with the right approach, every adult in society can learn to use a computer, even if only to a small extent, to enhance their experience of life. It just depends on how you, as a trainer, approach this.

Furthermore, as trainers, teachers or therapists; we have an obligation, both moral and legal, to teach people from all walks of life, in order to maximise their potential and encourage them back into education and promote lifelong learning.

This book contains practical information for trainers and therapists based on the experience of the authors.

Structure

The book is divided into 3 sections:

- Section 1 is about theory and we hope it has been presented in an easy-to-read way
- Section 2 contains session plans, schemes of work and training tips that are free to photocopy or reproduce by teachers or those using them in the course of their training work (further resources are available on the accompanying CD-ROM)
- Section 3 contains information that may be useful such as addresses, legislation, ICT examinations and qualifications, equipment and software, and internet links.

Accompanying CD-ROM

The accompanying disk contains 36 session plans, including tutor notes, schemes of work and ready-to-use resource materials. There are 12 session plans each for three different groups.

Using this book

The book is designed to be 'dipped into' rather than being read from cover to cover before use. Experienced tutors and trainers will be able to go directly to the section containing schemes of work and session plans and to the disk. Some readers may wish to read the theory section and others may want to look quickly at various sections to refer to information on a particular issue, such as assessment or information on different cultures.

Finally, we would like to thank you for buying the book and we hope it will really help you in your work and ultimately benefit the learner.

Taking the viewpoint of the learner

Perhaps one of the most important and useful approaches to teaching people with special needs is for the trainer to place the learner at the centre of the learning or therapeutic experience. Many trainers will do this instinctively and therapists often follow a person-centred practice philosophy. We have called this concept 'learner centredness'.

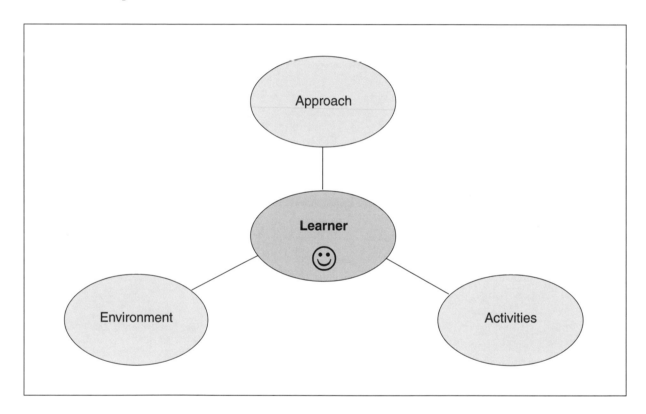

Figure 1. Placing the learner at the centre of the experience

'Learner centredness' relates to tailoring the learning experience to the learner. This is particularly important in teaching people with special needs as each individual will have their own unique needs, and their abilities are influenced by their illness or disability. This concept has been discussed extensively following a research project by Wertheimer (1997) which looked at learning opportunities for adults with mental health difficulties and emphasised participation and empowerment of learners.

Most colleges require that their learners have a written individual learning plan (ILP). In health settings, each patient (or service user) in a rehabilitation setting will have an individual intervention plan. Learner-centred thinking can help the formulation of both of these documents.

In Figure 1, three elements are seen to affect learning: approach; environment and activities. At the centre is the learner with his particular set of needs according to his level of ability and function.

The approach

The approach taken by a trainer will be successful if it relates to what the learner can deal with. This means the general, interpersonal style that the trainer adopts. A very directive approach, with a great deal of support and instruction from the trainer, may suit some learners. Others may respond better to minimal tutor involvement and a facilitatory style. In essence, we need to know how people learn to know how to train them better.

Confidentiality is an important aspect of working with people with special needs. Any disclosure by a person should be treated appropriately. Clearly information that may constitute a threat to self or others or is in breach of the law will need to be passed on to the appropriate person. This aspect should be communicated to learners in advance.

The environment

The environment will affect the learner and determine how easy it is for him to absorb and process information, depending on his needs. The environment of a busy group session may not suit a particular learner, and this will need to be considered. Colours and lighting in the room where a session is taking place may be either too stimulating or too relaxing. Space in the room can be calming for learners who do not like crowds but can cause anxiety for those who dislike open spaces.

For each session, the trainer needs to consider how a learner will respond to the learning environment and modify this if necessary and possible.

Activities

Activities in the session will need to be tailored to suit the needs of the learner and be achievable for them. If activities do not match a learner's level of function, the individual may not learn, may become disillusioned, or may even become agitated and distressed. Conversely, well-designed, graded activities will increase motivation and self-esteem. As the DFES 2003 strategy document, *Introducing Access for All*, says:

> Where teaching and learning are practical and skills are taught through activities *relevant to the learner*, success can be dramatic. [italics added]

Knowing the learner

Trainers are sometimes conditioned to expect more than may be possible for a learner with special needs. People from a teaching background may have often found that they are restricted by a curriculum or by external factors, such as funding and college requirements. Therapists may have found that bureaucratic requirements or limited funding affect their desire to give a client the quality and attention they really want to give.

Perhaps, however, one of the greatest changes anyone can make is in attitude and understanding, which in turn will have an influence on the organisations that constrain quality in learning and therapeutic work. This chapter presents some new ways of thinking about the learner and their needs and improving the quality of their experience.

Developmental theory and readiness to learn

To understand the learner, we need to understand more about how human beings develop. Normal human development occurs from birth in clear stages. As any human develops, they reach clearly defined 'milestones' in their understanding and mastery of the social and physical world around them.

One theory about illness or disability is that these cause people to either regress in their stages of psychosocial development or to not develop beyond a certain stage. This can be temporary (as with some mental illnesses or head injuries) or permanent (as with learning disabilities). The first group will advance again as they recover.

Sometimes, owing to physical damage, genetics or other reasons, a person cannot progress beyond a specific stage and never will. Therefore, any training will only ever be able to reach them at this level. Training here should really be aimed at maintaining skills rather than trying to develop them further.

Other theories suggest that people become mentally ill as a result of a failure to mature through developmental stages and that they need support and help to face these.

Knowing about these theories can assist a trainer in understanding why a learner will only be able to respond in certain ways.

Identifying stages of normal human development

Erik Erikson, a well-known psychologist, was one of the first theorists to describe human development. He identified eight stages (see Appendix A) of human psychosocial development where an individual has to resolve certain key challenges as they progress from birth to adulthood. Developmental psychology has grown from these ideas and those of other psychologists and psychoanalysts from the same era.

Erikson's ideas are useful because they highlight that human beings develop skills in natural, logical ways and that these stages cannot necessarily be forced.

This theory was taken forward by an occupational therapist in the USA, Anne Cronin Mosey, who developed a way of using developmental theory to form a practical system to help plan therapeutic sessions for people with special needs.

Mosey and the Seven Adaptive Skills

Mosey developed a practical theory for helping people with special needs to acquire the skills they need to live in the wider community. Her theory came to be known as Activities Therapy and described humans as possessing seven adaptive skills (most recently described in Chacksfield 2005). Each of these skills could be broken down into developmental stages, somewhat like Erikson's.

The value of Mosey's model is that, although it was initially designed for therapists, it can be used by trainers to plan ICT activities to meet the specific needs of an individual in a practical way. It can help trainers and therapists to understand why an individual might behave in a certain manner and to develop ways to change their learning experiences so that they get the most out of a session. A further benefit is that the model can be used without needing to know a diagnosis or classification of disability.

Mosey's system has two basic steps:

1. work out what level of function a person is at
2. design sessions to match their level.

As work progresses, reassessment shows progression or not, as the case may be, and allows for adjustment of session plans as required.

The Adaptive Skill system

In Mosey's theory, all human beings can be considered to have seven different skills that enable them to adapt to the world around them. When someone becomes ill, this affects their seven skills in different ways, which means that training or therapy has to be tailored according to what has happened to those skills.

Mosey's Seven Adaptive Skills are as follows:

1. perceptual motor skill – how people take in information from the environment, integrate it and act on it in a purposeful way, for example when using a mouse
2. cognitive skill – the way in which people organise thought and react as a result, such as when solving a problem
3. drive-object skill (needs, objects, drives) – the way people's motives affect what they do, such as expressing emotions verbally rather than breaking something angrily
4. dyadic interaction skill – the ability to interact with another person
5. group interaction skill – the ability to interact appropriately in a group of people
6. self-identity skill – how people see themselves
7. sexual identity skill – people's awareness of themselves as men or women and what this means in society, such as how to express their sexuality in an acceptable way.

Each skill can be divided up into sub-skills that relate to the level of function that a person is operating at, depending on their illness or disability (see Table 1.1). These sub-skills relate approximately to age-equivalent stages during human development. A person can act at different functional levels (sub-skills) for each skill depending on how their illness or disability affects them. The table lists these levels from lowest (least adaptive) to highest (most adaptive).

Assessment using the adaptive skills system

The way that the adaptive skills system can be used in assessment with adults with special needs is to provide them with an activity to do and observe how they respond. It doesn't matter about what the formal title of their illness or disability is as the focus is on how they function when doing an activity.

For users of this book, it will be important to consider how a person will need to interact *when using a computer* and this should be kept in mind when making an assessment.

It should be noted that this assessment is not quite the same as a standard educational assessment – it is more about the person and what they can realistically cope with in a learning environment.

For trainers and therapists the following approaches are recommended:

1. Obtain background information – obtain background information from other professionals that may know the learner.
2. Carry out an initial interview – a brief interview about how a person feels they cope with their world, their ideas about computers and ICT and how they feel they would cope with others in a learning situation.
3. Observe a task – provide them with a computer-based task that takes them from a basic to a more complex level and observe how far they progress, and their reactions. Further observation can be carried out in a group setting.

The person making the assessment should have a mental checklist that relates to the seven skills so they can estimate where a person is at in relation to these. A checklist is provided in Appendix B for this purpose. This may be adapted as necessary to suit the needs of the user.

Key areas

Not all skills will be applicable, depending on the learners that are being trained. Skills of particular importance are:

- dyadic interaction skill – how someone relates to individuals
- group interaction skill – how someone copes in a group setting
- cognitive skill – how someone thinks and reasons
- drive-object skill – how a person satisfies wants and needs.

Table 1.1 The Seven Adaptive Skills and their sub-skills

	Adaptive skill	Sub-skills
1	Perceptual motor skill (Useful for understanding physical responses in severely disabled individuals)	Can remain balanced when moving Can move both sides of the body appropriately and respond to sounds Can perceive the body in the environment and use body parts appropriately Can move in a coordinated way and understand sounds and language Can tell the difference between right and left and remember sounds and words Can use abstract ideas, can understand more complex language and give feedback
2	Cognitive skill (Useful for assessing ability to process information and identifying how best to present tasks)	Can use instinctive behaviour patterns to interact with the world Can make use of vision, touch, hearing and taste in a coordinated way Can observe and remember interactions with the environment and put responses into sequence Can set goals and act on these, can see people and things as separate from self, can imitate and learn from others Can solve problems by trial and error and can watch and learn from observations Can remember how experiences felt, can tell the difference between thought and action and know that everything needs a cause Can name and classify objects, can hold a balanced view of all aspects of an object and understand the views of others Can think flexibly, use logic and ideas or theories
3	Drive-object skill (NB The ability to tolerate a delay in satisfaction is important in this skill. This varies across all the sub-skills. These criteria are useful in understanding tolerance with an activity and ability to deal with frustration)	Can obtain satisfaction from people or things for short periods of time Can maintain satisfaction with one primary person or thing and continue this over time Can express anger/frustration in a way that leads to satisfaction Can transfer ability to obtain satisfaction from people or things other than the primary one Can create imaginary objects and can control anger/frustration Can obtain results by using one object (recognising its strengths and limitations) or from a variety of objects
4	Dyadic interaction skill (Useful in assessing ability to relate to others)	Can enter an association relationship (i.e. acquaintances) Can interact in an authority relationship (accept training) Can enter a friendship Can enter peer-authority relationships (other learners can help) Can enter an intimate relationship (close friend) Can engage in nurturing relationships (supportive)
5	Group interaction skill (Useful in identifying the extent to which a person can participate in a group activity)	Can participate in a parallel group (same room as others but limited interaction) Can participate in a project group (shared task that is directed by trainer) Can participate in an egocentric cooperative group (interacts and initiates activity in a group with trainer direction) Can participate in a cooperative group (interacts and influences group to achieve goals with support from trainer) Can participate in a mature group (self-directed group session)
6	Self-identity skill (Useful for assessing self-esteem, self-awareness and self-efficacy)	Can see self as a worthy object Knows own assets and limitations Can see self as self-directed Can see self as a productive, contributing member of society Can see self in more depth Can accept change associated with age
7	Sexual identity skill (Useful for assessing if someone can cope with others they may be attracted to, challenging behaviour and lack of confidence about sexuality)	Can accept self as male or female Accepts sexual maturation as positive Can have a meaningful sexual relationship appropriately Can maintain a sexual relationship Can accept later-life sexual changes (e.g. menopause)

An assessment will help the trainer identify a learner's sub-skill level for each of these and they will know what to expect during the learning process.

The seven skills are helpful when a learner has difficulty coping in a learning situation. It may be that materials or learning tasks have been pitched at too high a level for the person's ability.

Planning sessions using the adaptive skills system

Once an assessment has been carried out and the levels of function have been identified using the sub-skills, the learning tasks can be planned. It does not matter what the special needs are because the adaptive skills structure focuses on how needs affect performance.

The examples below show how the concept works. Chapter 3 describes activity planning in more depth.

Steve

Steve wants to take part in an ICT session. Brenda, the trainer, is aware that he has some special needs but is not sure how these might affect his ability to take part in activities. Brenda asks him to sit at a computer and type his name. He finds great difficulty in recognising letters and does not achieve this. Brenda realises that Steve is at a low level in his cognitive skill (can imitate and learn from others). In her mind, she analyses the stages in using a keyboard and starts by teaching him to recognise letters on the keys. She then gets him to sequence by asking him to copy simple text that is written in a font (Arial, capitals) that is similar to the letters on the keyboard he is using. Steve gradually progresses to the next cognitive skill level in relation to the keyboard.

Anna

Before Anna was in hospital, she was a journalist and worked on a local newspaper. She became mentally unwell and was unable to do her job. She has come to the ICT sessions to build her confidence again. Graham, a trainer, asks Anna to type her name. She does this without a problem. He then asks her to do a word-search. She frequently asks for help and when she cannot complete the task becomes upset, frustrated and angry. Graham gives her an easier task that she can achieve. Graham realises that, as a result of her mental illness, Anna is at a low drive-object level (can maintain satisfaction with one primary person or thing and continue this over time) and he will have to make learning tasks simpler and in clear steps until she can cope with more complex tasks. The fact that she was a journalist in the past does not mean it can be assumed that she will be able to operate at a high functional level while she is unwell.

Use of the Seven Adaptive Skills system can greatly assist learner centredness and the development of individual learning plans or intervention plans.

Assessing and evaluating – general issues

Assessment is part of ensuring training content is delivered in the most appropriate way to the learner. Assessment can be informal, such as when the trainer or therapist continually assesses their students during their learning. Formal assessment consists of procedures that may involve interviews, questionnaires, and observation of a learner performing a task.

For adults with special needs, formal assessment covers two areas:

1. assessment of ability
2. assessment of their level of ICT knowledge.

Assessment of ability

A person is likely to find that their special needs will impact on their ability to learn. It is useful for the trainer to gather knowledge about ability in order to ensure that they adapt training activities appropriately.

The ability to learn can be affected by the symptoms of a mental illness (such as schizophrenia), or the limitations caused by a learning disability (such as Down's syndrome) or brain damage (perhaps caused by alcohol misuse or a traffic accident). Sometimes the medication a person has to take because of a mental illness will also affect their ability to engage in an activity, possibly owing to side effects. Sometimes a person may have used illegal drugs before coming to a session and this may affect their performance. If this is suspected it may be worth seeking advice from a manager or a health professional working with the learner. Health issues can be present, such as epilepsy, which is worth knowing about in case a person becomes unwell during a session. It is important to be aware of procedures for managing this kind of incident. Other issues can also be present, such as literacy and numeracy, which if they present severe difficulties may need to be discussed with a basic skills tutor.

Most commonly, all the above factors will cause a person to have difficulties concentrating, processing information, coping with emotions, and coping with the environment (social and physical). Colleges will often be able to provide diagnostic assessments to identify literacy and numeracy issues.

Learners that have come from a healthcare environment will have had assessments within this setting. If permission is given, it can be useful to make use of these assessments when discussing specific needs with a learner and their carer.

Interviews

Holding an interview with a potential learner is useful prior to commencement of the course. This can help the trainer 'get a feel' for the student's ability, motivation and attitudes to the learning situation. It may also be worth interviewing a carer or relative, if this is appropriate.

Assessment approaches

Basic analytical tools can include checklists to prompt the trainer to gather information or for a professional to complete with basic information about the learner. In healthcare settings a referral form is commonly used for this purpose.

Confidentiality

If in a health setting, confidentiality is important and no personal information should be discussed outside the centre or setting without the individual learner's consent.

Assessment of level of ICT knowledge

Assessing a person's level of ICT knowledge is useful in assisting them to identify realistic goals but also for the trainer to understand the input required.

An exception is where a learner had gained a high level of ICT knowledge prior to the onset of their illness or disability. An example might be someone who used to be an ICT professional who later developed manic depression or suffered brain damage and lost their ability. For these students the level of knowledge can remain to a certain extent, but their illness or condition may prevent them from functioning as they used to. This can be frustrating for them and a trainer will need to be aware of this.

Assessment of level of knowledge can be done via:

- interview – asking them what they know about the subject, past training, etc.
- observation – of a task to see how far they progress with it
- questionnaires – the learner can answer questions about the subject.

Assessment will then enable clear plans to be made.

Planning

Within further education colleges, learners are expected to write an individual learning plan (ILP) with their tutor. This relates to the specific learning tasks that the student will undergo during a course and an agreement on participation.

Example – Passport to Learning

The London Borough of Tower Hamlets Lifelong Learning service in East London has developed the Passport to Learning, which enables a person to produce a portfolio to record their own experiences, life skills, and educational experience -- a record of achievement. This encourages reflection and adaptation of skills for all members of the community. It also enables access to further courses and development within the adult education and employment system.

Within health settings, most learners who are also patients will have an individual care plan or intervention plan. Much of this will relate to their condition, but for occupational therapy the plan will often be around lifestyle and developing skills for daily life.

Example – The Education Link Team

The Education Link Team in Birmingham (Westwood 2003) is managed within a mental health NHS trust and sets up partnerships with various agencies with the aim of providing courses that have support for adults with mental health needs. Support is individualised and planned through advice and guidance sessions. Such individualised support enables learners to take steps to access education in a way that suits their own particular needs, which in turn builds their confidence and supports them to take control of their learning.

2

Breaking down tasks – differentiation and grading

The concepts of differentiation and grading are useful because they help with planning sessions. Differentiation provides some good general principles about creating the right learning experiences for the individual in relation to a curriculum. Grading looks specifically at an activity and what it can do for a person in relation to their functional ability. Combining both concepts can maximise the effectiveness of work with adults who have special needs in an ICT environment. Differentiation can help in planning a series of sessions with a given course. Activity analysis of computer equipment and software can put these 'under the microscope' and ensure that they are used to the greatest effect. Both differentiation and grading are common sense and many trainers and therapists do what they describe anyway.

Differentiation

Curriculum differentiation is a broad term referring to the need to tailor training environments, course plans and training practices to create appropriately different learning experiences for mixed-ability learners within a curriculum. Differentiation is the adjustment of the training process according to the different levels and learning needs of the learners. It can be aimed at:

- a whole group
- small groups within the larger learning group
- individuals.

There is a wide range of theory about differentiation. However, the following six principles from Carol Tomlinson (1995), who is considered by some to be the 'guru' of differentiation, sum up much of the thinking.

Six principles of good differentiation:

- proactive – i.e. trainers assume that learners are different
- more qualitative than quantitative – trainers adjust the nature of tasks, not the quantity
- relies upon multiple approaches to content, process, and products
- focuses upon students – learning is 'engaging, relevant and interesting'
- blends whole-group, small-group and individual instruction – there is a flow to instruction that creates a rhythmic pattern between whole-group, small-group and individual learning experiences
- organic – simply meaning learners and trainers are learning simultaneously.

Activity analysis and grading

Grading, a similar concept to differentiation, is used by occupational therapists within healthcare settings. It refers to the extent to which an activity can be adapted to allow for change in the person doing it. In order to identify potential for grading, the process of activity analysis has to occur.

Activity analysis consists of examining the components of any activity, and the demands it makes, in order to assess its potential for use with a particular individual. According to occupational therapist Jennifer Creek (2003), analysis of an activity enables a therapist or trainer to:

- understand the demands that the activity will place on the individual in terms of the range of skills required for its performance
- assess what needs the activity might satisfy
- determine the extent to which it might inhibit undesirable behaviour
- determine whether or not the activity is within the client's capacity
- discover the skills the activity will develop in the client – these may be specific skills such as using a mouse or more general, transferable skills such as changing the appearance of text in a word processor
- provide a basis for adapting and grading activities to meet particular ends
- synthesise new activities to meet particular goals – elements from different activities can be combined to create new activities that best meet the needs of the client.

According to Creek, the domains of activity analysis include:

- physical
- cognitive
- psychological
- interpersonal.

The basis of an activity

An activity is made up of tasks – any activity can be divided up into separate tasks or steps (see example in Table 2.1). For example, production of a letter involves turning the computer on, using the mouse to start the word processor, typing, editing, formatting the text, saving the document, and printing the document.

Table 2.1 Some aspects of using a computer

Physical	Cognitive	Psychological	Interpersonal
Posture	Attention	Expression of feelings	Individual or group
Range of movement	Concentration	Control of feelings	Communication
Types of movement	Choice	Frustration tolerance	Cooperation
Judgement	Abstract thinking	Expression of needs	Structure
Mobility	Reading	Gratification of needs	Social rules
	Typing	Independence	Involvement
	Following demonstration/advice		
	Speed		
	Memory		

Steps or tasks within an activity can be further divided into smaller steps and tasks. How much detail is needed will depend on how difficult someone finds a task. Each of the aspects of the activity above could be broken down to its specific steps, such as use of the mouse (Table 2.2).

Clearly, if someone has special needs that inhibit their abilities in these areas, they will need support and assistance to achieve their goals. Sometimes an activity will need to be adapted to enable someone to learn. Session plans should add in activities that are relevant to a person's ability and not set unachievable goals. Activity analysis is a way of knowing the demands a task can make on a person. For each of these stages, an activity can be planned to enable the individual to practise and learn the skills needed for each stage.

For experienced trainers or therapists, activity analysis will become common sense.

Table 2.2 Elements involved in using the mouse

Step	Physical	Cognitive	Psychological	Interpersonal
1. Hand position	Sensation, grip	Understanding instructions, concentration, memory	Control of feelings, involvement	Individual interaction, communication, cooperation
2. Lateral movement	Perception, motor planning, motor coordination	Following demonstration/advice, concentration	Involvement, control of feelings, playing/exploring	As above plus involvement, structure
3. Relating mouse movement to cursor symbol	As above	Abstract thinking, concentration, perceiving cause and effect	As above plus frustration tolerance	As above
4. Use of buttons	As above	Concentration, perceiving cause and effect	As above	As above
5. Holding buttons to highlight text	As above	As above	As above plus trust, independence	As above
6. Use of wheel (if applicable)	As above	As above	As above	As above

Grading

Once an activity has been analysed it is easy to grade it so that a person can carry it out step by step, according to their functional ability. This concept is similar to differentiation in that a trainer can plan different activities for different learners according to their needs. Grading allows the demands of the activity on the learner to be tailored to meet the needs of an individual in a very direct way.

Group versus individual learning

Depending on a learner's ability to cope in a group setting, their needs may be best met either on an individual, one-to-one basis or within a group. A great deal of information is available on group work so this will not be explored in detail here. The main advantages of groups are that:

- more people can benefit from learning at once
- they can be more cost effective in the use of staff time
- they can develop skills through shared experience and social interaction.

However, groups may not be an appropriate way for people of very different levels of ability to learn as a trainer may not always be able to divide attention between the different needs of individuals. Some learners cannot tolerate groups at all and become stressed in group-learning situations. The adaptive skills approach is very useful in planning group sessions to account for different needs of individuals (see Chapter 1).

3

Understanding stress and anxiety

An issue that can affect how a person learns is their level of stress or anxiety when in a learning environment. It is recognised that a small amount of anxiety can increase performance. However, when this is too great, a learner's ability to absorb information and to be motivated can be adversely affected. In some people, stress can cause their illness or disability to worsen and awareness of this is an important part of risk management, particularly for people with identified mental health needs.

The good news is that anxiety and stress can be understood and strategies can be developed to manage this and to help learners cope within their learning environment. Clearly, there is also value in the trainer's learning about their own stress and being able to manage this as a general life skill.

Theory: the fight or flight mechanism

The psychological theory known as the 'fight or flight' mechanism has been developed to explain how human beings react to stressful situations. This originates from the early stages of human evolution and is a basic survival mechanism. In summary, the human brain and body react to a stressful stimulus by preparing to either fight or run away. This was useful in early times as the stressful stimulus would often be a predator or a rival human. The body would therefore prepare to fight or to run away as fast as possible.

Modern sources of stress are obviously less likely to be aggressive animals and are more likely to be situations such as traffic jams, the pressure of constant work, frustrating interactions or shocks, worries and fears. Sometimes even a good idea can cause us uncertainty and lead to a stress reaction. Nevertheless, these stimuli all trigger the body's fight or flight reaction and sometimes leave us in a permanent state of stress.

The fight or flight reaction causes the human body to prepare itself in a number of ways, with physical effects that include the following:

- increased heart-rate, to provide more blood to muscles
- transfer of blood from stomach and digestive system to muscles
- production of chemicals, such as adrenaline, to increase ability to move
- production of endorphins to reduce pain experienced as a result of muscle tension or injury
- shut-down of nonessential systems, such as the stomach, to divert all energy to physical action
- heightened visual and sensory awareness
- increased sweating to cool the body during action.

Some of the ways this will be felt physically by the person are:

- faster heartbeat
- faster breathing
- dry mouth
- red face
- muscle tension

- 'butterflies' in the stomach
- sweaty palms
- feeling the need to 'do something'
- feeling anger or fear
- loosening of the bladder or bowel in extreme situations.

The fight or flight reaction essentially produces a large amount of energy that needs to be expended. Clearly, if the situation leads to physical exertion, such as running, then this energy would be used up. As most of the triggers to this reaction nowadays cannot be dealt with by running or fighting, the body often cannot use up the energy it has generated, and the chemicals (such as adrenaline or endorphins) that have been created, resulting in illness, stress or anxiety.

Prolonged stress can lead to quite severe illness, including depression, chronic anxiety, panic attacks, heart problems and stomach problems. This idea has been famously described by Hans Selye (1946) who identified the General Adaptation Syndrome (GAS), which results from prolonged stress. The GAS has three stages:

- alarm – the immediate response of the fight or flight reaction leading to suppression of the immune system
- resistance – initial resistance to disease as the immune system steps up its response and overworks
- exhaustion – when the body is unable to maintain the high level of stress and health starts to deteriorate.

Anxiety and stress in disabled learners

Anxiety and stress can be experienced by people with disabilities as much as any other people. However, sometimes someone's specific needs mean they are not always able to express their feelings clearly. It is important to be aware of this in a learning situation as some learning activities may trigger their fight or flight reaction. This could be for several reasons, such as a learning activity may feature a picture or concept that has caused anxiety for the learner in the past, or a learner may simply be unable to tolerate the activity.

The way a learner's disability or illness operates may affect their ability and tolerance of stress. Sometimes this can be because their disability has occurred as a result of severe stress and additional stress is thus not helpful. Sometimes their bodies are generally less able to tolerate stress. Sometimes the condition itself, such as the hallucinations that some people experience in schizophrenia, may make someone feel stressed.

Awareness by a trainer or staff member can help prevent any difficulties arising from a stress reaction. This, once again, highlights the need to know your student and to obtain further information from carers or support staff where possible. Sometimes a disabled student may be unable to express their anxiety so the trainer will need to recognise signs of a reaction in order to be aware if a person's tolerance for a situation is being affected.

Stress signs are as listed above. If a trainer is aware of these they can attempt to help the person reduce their reaction. The fight or flight reaction may stop a person thinking straight and may even lead them to run away or become aggressive and unpredictable.

Managing stress and anxiety

Trainers or therapists can best manage stress using three approaches:

- knowledge
- prevention
- early intervention.

Knowledge

Knowing about stress, the fight or flight reaction and how this operates for a particular learner is the first step. It is important for any trainers to obtain relevant information about what triggers stress reactions in a particular learner, their ability to tolerate stressful situations and strategies that have helped them manage this in the past.

Prevention

Setting up the learning environment so that it is relaxed, calming and students feel safe and that they can learn at their own pace can prevent stress occurring. It is advisable for a trainer to have strategies or other exercises or ways of explaining learning tasks. This is useful if, for example, a learner becomes frustrated with a particular task and needs another approach.

Stating clearly to learners at the beginning of a session that if they find things difficult they can stop or take time out is important. Doing this ensures they feel safe and confident in the trainer. ICT tasks in particular can become frustrating, such as when data is lost or someone is unable to grasp a concept about a computer and apply it as quickly as others.

Feedback to carers, support staff or a clinical team is important if a person appears to find difficulty with learning activities and appears to be stressed, especially if it occurs on a regular basis.

Thinking about possible causes of stress and how to reduce these within a session will make it more productive for those involved. Clearly, a good assessment of a learner's needs and functional ability is an effective way of ensuring that activities within session do not cause undue stress. Awareness of ways to make things easier is useful and there are many ways this can be done. Tips, such as the effects of colour and typeface in resource materials, awareness of cultural issues and knowledge of risk assessment, can be useful in reducing stress or learner anxiety. Some of these issues are explored in Chapter 4.

Early intervention

If someone becomes stressed or anxious during a session, there are some clear strategies you can take to deal with the situation. These include:

- reassurance – talking calmly with the person and helping them either express their feelings or solve the problem that has distressed them
- changing an activity – it could be that a learning activity is too much for someone to cope with, and changing this can thus reduce stress
- time out – suggesting that the person takes time away from the session can help, and (if possible) enabling them to talk to another staff member or carer about what is troubling them.

At the end of a session it is worth spending some time evaluating the event and planning with the person how problems could be prevented in future sessions.

In general, it is important to know about the learner and their needs. This will prevent stress and anxiety occurring.

4

Special issues

Risk and safety

Risk and safety are important concepts when working with adults with special needs. Although these issues relate to all learners, some special considerations are important with this group.

Health and safety is a major concern in the workplace and is as relevant in learning environments as in any other. Most countries have legislation about risk and what workers and employers are required to do. Health and safety is basically about preventing people from being harmed at work or becoming ill by taking the right precautions and providing a satisfactory working environment.

Risk is the concept used to describe what might cause harm or illness. Risk assessment essentially means a careful examination of what, in your work, could cause harm to people, so that you can weigh up whether you have taken enough precautions or should do more to prevent harm.

In some special needs groups who may be considered to behave in a challenging or unpredictable way, it is sometimes important to be aware of personal safety. This aspect is discussed below. It is important to find out about policies and procedures in environments where personal safety is a potential issue.

Assessing risk in the learning environment

Any trainer or therapist working in a learning or clinical environment will need to be aware of hazards that lead to a risk. ICT environments, for example, may have hazards such as trailing cables that anyone in the room could trip over. A risk assessment would highlight this so that it can be dealt with, perhaps by covering or re-routeing the cables to reduce the risk. A trainer may work in various learning environments and so should ideally risk assess each one separately and ask people who work there about any potential risks.

The British government (Health and Safety Executive 1999) suggests five steps to risk assessment:

1. Look for the hazards.
2. Decide who might be harmed and how.
3. Evaluate the risks and decide whether the existing precautions are adequate or whether more should be done.
4. Record your findings.
5. Review your assessment and revise it if necessary.

You should report any risks that you are concerned about to the person in charge of the place you are working in. A form that you can copy and use to record your risk assessment is provided in Table 4.1.

Hazards that are often particularly relevant to ICT learning environments include:

- trailing cables
- electrical sockets overloaded (too many plugs in one socket)
- crowded room
- blocked fire exits

Table 4.1 Risk assessment form

RISK ASSESSMENT		
Name of learning/clinical environment being risk assessed:	Date assessed:	
	Carried out by:	
Address:	Signed:	
	Review date:	
Significant hazards	**Groups of people who are at risk from the hazards you have identified**	**Existing precautions or location of information, any risks that are not controlled adequately, any recommendations**

- damaged equipment
- visual display units (VDUs) – see below and Appendix C
- use of equipment by people who are not trained to do so
- positioning of people at desks – right height, back strain, wrist strain, etc.
- loose or damaged flooring
- poor lighting
- low temperature
- poor ventilation

- storage of inks and printing materials
- storage of files, books and equipment
- heavy loads to carry, for example computer equipment
- other hazards, depending on the environment.

Visual display units

Most learning centres and clinical environments will have a specific policy about visual display units (VDUs) or monitors. In some countries there are specific regulations about working with VDUs. Some of the advice below is adapted from the British guidance (Health and Safety Executive 2003).

VDUs generally include a display screen (either standard television-style or flat screen or portable computer screens), usually forming part of a computer and showing text, numbers and graphics. Some users may get aches and pains in their hands, wrists, arms, neck, shoulders or back, especially after long periods of uninterrupted VDU work. Sometimes people can report aches and pains due to feeling stressed.

Problems can often be avoided by good workplace design, so that you can work comfortably, and by good working practices (such as taking frequent short breaks from the VDU).

Stress from VDU working can generally be avoided by ensuring tasks are not too difficult for the person doing them.

According to UK guidelines, extensive research has found no evidence that VDUs can cause disease or permanent damage to eyes. However, long spells of VDU work can lead to tired eyes and discomfort and people who wear contact lenses may find their eyes can get dry as a result of the environment they are working in.

Headaches may result from several things that occur with VDU work, such as:

- screen glare
- poor image quality
- a need for different spectacles
- stress from the pace of work
- anxiety about new technology
- reading the screen for long periods without a break
- poor posture
- a combination of these.

It is known to be unlikely that epileptic fits can be triggered by working at VDU screens.

Laptops and portable computers

The design of laptops and portable computers usually means they are smaller than standard desktop computers. When using laptops it is important to sit comfortably, angle the screen to minimise screen glare and take frequent breaks. It is probably better to use a desktop computer whenever this is possible.

Using the mouse

Intensive use of a mouse may lead to aches and pains. If this happens it is worth changing the position of the mouse and making sure that frequent breaks are taken. The mouse should be placed close to the person using a computer so it can be used with a relaxed arm and a straight wrist, to minimise discomfort. Sometimes people use alternative devices, such as a trackball, if they find these more comfortable.

General issues

In general, it is important to analyse and risk assess the whole workstation, including the equipment, furniture and the work environment. In some countries, this is a legal requirement, as is the provision of the right types of adjustable chair and lighting. Trainers and therapists should plan work on computers to include breaks, and changes in the type of work.

Appendix C provides further guidance on safe and comfortable use of computer equipment.

Fire

It is important for all staff in a particular building to find out about any fire procedures and rules, and the locations of fire exits and equipment. You should also inform your learners and/or their carers about this.

First aid

It is advisable to either have a basic first aid certificate or to know who the person to contact for first aid is within the learning centre or clinical environment. In some countries, you can also study for a more comprehensive First Aid at Work certificate.

Manual handling

If anyone has to carry computer equipment or move it from one place to another, they can risk causing pain or harm to their back. Some countries have manual handling regulations which state that anyone who is likely to handle heavy loads learns to do so safely. In general, it is important to ensure you know how to handle a heavy load or if in doubt ask for help from someone who does. It is advisable not to allow learners to handle heavy loads.

Special situations and risk management

Certain centres may specialise in helping adults with challenging needs and behavioural problems. These can include what are sometimes called challenging behaviour units, psychiatric intensive care units, forensic mental health units and possibly prisons.

Although learners/patients in these units can at first seem to be a frightening group to work with, as long as you follow the rules and work with the centre, it is very unlikely that any problems will occur. Anyone who is expected to work in these units should be provided with a formal induction that explains any special rules or issues with people using those services, i.e. the patients or learners. *It is important that people at the centre or unit tell you about any risk issues or problems that might arise for each individual attending a session.*

A trainer or therapist will sometimes be asked to take part in additional training in relation to safety, such as de-escalation skills (how to talk to someone who may be distressed or aggressive and calm them down) and breakaway techniques (how to escape a difficult situation). It is advisable to ensure that your employer or line manager allows paid time to attend this training.

It may be a requirement that an additional member of staff from the unit or centre stays in the room when a session is in progress. This is to be encouraged as that person can help in an emergency.

You will be asked to provide feedback on how individual learners have behaved within a session. This may include asking you to provide written feedback, and it should be included in your paid teaching time. It is important to agree this prior to starting within the unit.

The manager may suggest that you will need 'supervision'. For trainers not used to this concept, this means regular meetings for support where you and a nominated member of staff can discuss how sessions are going, how learners are responding, and any problems. This is designed to help ensure your safety and to help the staff in the unit work better with their service users.

In general, if you are a working in one of these units and feel uncomfortable, do talk with your manager and/or the centre staff.

Some tips include:

- if appropriate, have someone with you for safety
- know exits and alarms
- make sure you work so that you are near the exit
- know important procedures
- meet the manager responsible for the learning or clinical environment
- familiarise yourself with the environment
- know which person to feed back students' behaviour to
- if you need to write notes, get someone to show you the system
- ensure your employer or line manager knows your needs in the centre
- agree funded time for any extra duties and training specific to the centre/unit
- inform the nominated supervisor or centre manager of any problems or concerns as soon as possible
- ensure you keep a professional distance with learners
- ensure you understand how stress and anxiety work and how to deal with this (see Chapter 3).

Different cultures and special needs

Equality of opportunity is important not only in relation to special needs but also to the culture from which a person originates or with which they feel they are most affiliated. Although many cultures are based on religious ideals, a person's culture can be quite separate from their religion. Religion does not presuppose culture.

It is useful for trainers to understand some of the aspects of culture in order to make the best use of learning opportunities, to ensure they approach the learner with tact, and to understand any specific cultural needs of a learner.

The main aspects of culture that will be considered in relation to learning include:

- religion
- traditions from a country of origin
- social rules and skills relating to the culture a person feels most affiliated with
- symbols and images
- clothing and dress rules
- festivals

Religion

Religion is a major aspect of culture. The major religions in the world today are usually considered to be (in alphabetical order):

- Christianity – Catholic, Russian and Greek Orthodox and Protestant
- Buddhism – including Mahayana, Theravada and Zen
- Hinduism – Vaishnavism and Shaivism, each of which includes many different traditions and sects
- Islam – branches include Sunni, Shiite and Sufi
- Judaism – main branches include Ashkenazic, Sephardic, Orthodox
- Paganism – main branches include Wicca, Druidism and Asatru
- Sikh – main branches are Udasis, Sahajdharis, The Khalsa.

There are many branches of these main religions, other smaller religions and even a range of newer religious traditions. If you know you are going to be working with people from a particular culture or religious background, it is worth finding out more before you start.

Culture

Traditions from country of origin also form part of a culture.

Information about the cultural backgrounds of learners is often collected by colleges, healthcare centres and other organisations in order to ensure cultural needs are being met effectively. Most organisations will have equal opportunity policies that describe their approach to ensuring people are treated as equal regardless of culture, race, religion, ability, sexuality, gender, residency status and other issues.

Racism is a major form of discrimination and the concept of institutional racism is being dealt with by many large organisations. Institutional racism describes discrimination on the grounds of race or culture that is not deliberate but is inherent because of attitudes and practices. Some of the attitudes and practices within an organisation, though discriminatory, may be based on outdated concepts and have become habitual.

Recent legislation in Europe and other countries has addressed discrimination on the grounds of disability. Section 3 provides information on the laws in various countries.

Cultural awareness

It is important for any trainer or therapist to develop their cultural awareness and find out about the people they are working with. Some culturally focused learning centres may have codes of practice that relate to specific groups that the trainer is not aware of. If in doubt, ask.

Examples of issues that have occurred to trainers known to the authors:

- Jewish women's group – the (female) trainer was asked to wear a skirt as trousers are not seen as acceptable by the women in the session.
- Muslim women – the (female) trainer was asked to cover her hair out of respect for the cultural wishes of the group. Another trainer was asked to have a break in a session so learners could attend a prayer session.
- Asylum seekers family session – the trainer had to adapt teaching to the needs of mothers who had their children with them in the classroom. Asylum seekers attending the session had limited childcare options. The trainer was able to be flexible and alter her approach to accommodate family learning.

Culture is clearly an important issue and needs to be given adequate attention in relation to learners with special needs as much as anyone else.

Management issues

Management issues will come to the fore when implementing some of the recommendations for adapting methods and environments for learning in relation to adults with special needs. In relation to ICT equipment this has cost implications and must be considered if an effective service is to be run. It is a whole new approach in special needs requiring flexibility, funding and firm commitment.

It is worth the time and effort for a manager to go and spend time in the setting where the trainers are working. This can give a real perspective on the issues faced by trainers on a day-to-day basis. Some managers will return to the 'treadmill' and lead a few sessions as they recognise that time away from practice can deskill them.

Some of the management issues that often arise include:

- Budgets and buying equipment – as well as the normal budget for ICT, extra funds will be required for special needs equipment and resources, specialist software and hardware.
- Extra paid time may be required as special needs trainers will have to put in considerably more time in preparation and student assessment than a conventional trainer working with mainstream adult learners.
- Flexibility in timing of courses to allow for late starts or late finishes: late starts may be necessary in order to allow for assessment time; late finishes may be necessary where students progress at a slower pace than anticipated or to spend extra time carrying out evaluations.
- Flexibility in course outcomes. For many students, attendance at a course and the taking part is a significant achievement. This may not meet the conventional needs of a college where registers and good exam results are of high importance. It may be useful for a manager to visit the centre where adults with special needs are being trained and discuss any issues with other managers. This is particularly important in the NHS.
- Good ICT support. For special needs it will be important for managers to prioritise technical support in terms of maintaining equipment and installing adapted equipment and software. Reliable and speedy responses to requests are important because of the effect on learners. This may be particularly so where learners have difficulty concentrating or maintaining engagement in a learning situation because of their special needs.
- Training opportunities for trainers. Tutors and trainers will need additional training themselves to keep up to date with specialist software and equipment, students' disabilities and illnesses and assessment approaches.

In most learning environments, training in safety and risk, fire regulations, moving and handling and conflict management are important.

Health and safety regulations

VDUs

In some countries, employers have to provide training to make sure employees can use their VDU and workstation safely, and know how to make best use of them to avoid health problems, for example by adjusting the chair. It is advised that this is done for trainers and therapists who can then make sure their learners are safe.

Working with NHS policies

When a trainer is visiting an NHS centre from a college and teaching patients, there will be policies unique to the NHS organisation that have to be taken into account. Some policies will require any staff working in a hospital environment to attend health and safety training of various sorts. This time may need to be paid for by the college or negotiated as time paid by the NHS organisation. A particular example might be courses around management of aggressive behaviour, such as within a secure mental health unit or a prison environment. These courses are mandatory and considered a high priority to ensure staff safety.

In general, good management support is crucial to the success of special needs training for adults. This may be more important if training occurs in centres away from a college campus, hospital environments or specialist units. In order to make training as accessible as possible for learners with special needs, backing for trainers from managers is essential in ensuring flexibility, funding and firm commitment.

What to do if . . . ?

It is hard to anticipate what may happen in a learning situation and this section attempts to cover some of the possibilities. The examples below are based on real experiences.

Table 4.2 What to do if . . . ?

Situation	Possible cause	Solution
A learner comes with their carer and the carer is constantly interrupting the trainer.	The carer is concerned and wants to make sure their person is looked after in the classroom, and does not realise their interruption is unhelpful.	In a break, the trainer could take the carer to one side and reassure them and ask them politely not to interrupt.
A learner tells the trainer to get out of the class because she is wearing trousers.	The learner was in a class of Jewish women and part of their cultural belief is that women should only wear skirts.	The trainer made sure they were aware of cultural needs next time by asking the centre staff.
A carer is very demanding of the students, telling them what to do rather than allowing the student to learn of their own accord. This was contrary to the trainer's approach.	The carer did not know about the way in which the trainer had hoped to work.	Discuss with the carers the best way to work together and make an agreement about this. If the difficulty continues, it may be necessary to involve management from the centre and from the college or hospital unit.
A student becomes very attached to the trainer/therapist. S/he spends more time in lessons than necessary, is over-friendly with the trainer, relies on them for advice, and finds reasons to get the trainer to talk to them more.	The learner in this situation has a 'crush' or a transferred dependency on the trainer.	The trainer discussed this in supervision and informed the learner's key worker. A plan was made to ensure professional boundaries could be maintained. All advice sessions were done with the key worker present. The trainer monitored the situation. The key worker addressed the issues behind the situation with the learner.
A trainer goes to a forensic mental health unit wearing a short skirt and leggings. She is asked to return home and change.	The trainer is wearing what she would normally wear at work.	She was asked to change because she could put herself at risk because of some of the challenging needs of the clients.
A trainer is in a forensic mental health unit and keeps being left on her own with learners.	The forensic unit staff were called to other duties and had failed to ensure they replaced the staff in the teaching sessions.	The trainer informed the line manager, who contacted the forensic unit. The college withdrew the tutor until the situation had been resolved and a formal agreement was drawn up between the unit and the college.
The trainer feels lack of support from the centre in terms of further training and resources to adequately carry out her role.	The line manager was unaware of the extra support needed by the trainer.	The trainer contacted the line manager to discuss options. The manager asked within the college if there was further funding to help develop this area of work. Further training was written into the trainer's personal development plan.

References

Chacksfield, J. (2005) 'Activities Therapy: Recapitulation of Ontogenesis', in Duncan, E. and Hagedorn, R. (eds) *Foundations for Practice*. London: Elsevier, in press.

Creek, J. (2001) *Occupational Therapy and Mental Health*, 3rd edition. Edinburgh: Churchill Livingstone.

Department for Education and Skills (2001) *Special Educational Needs and Disability Act*. London: DFES.

DFES (2003) *Introducing Access for All: Supporting Learners with Learning Difficulties and Disabilities Across the Curriculum*. London: DFES.

Department of Health (2001) *Valuing People: A New Strategy for Learning Disability for the 21st Century*. London: DH.

Erikson, E. H. and Erikson, J. M. (1987) *The Life Cycle Completed*. New York: W.W. Norton & Co.

Health and Safety Executive (HSE) (1999) *Five Steps to Risk Assessment*. London: HSE.

Health and Safety Executive (HSE) (2003) *Working with VDUs*. London: HSE.

Office of the Deputy Prime Minister (2004) *Mental Health and Social Exclusion*. London: ODPM.

Selye, H. (1946) 'The general adaptation syndrome and the diseases of adaptation', *Journal of Clinical Endocrinology*, **6**, 117–230.

Tomlinson, C. A. (1995) *How to Differentiate Instruction in Mixed-Ability Classrooms*. Alexandria, VA: Association for Supervision and Curriculum Development (ASCD).

Wertheimer, A. (1997) *Images of Possibility: Creating Learning Opportunities for Adults with Mental Health Difficulties*. Leicester: National Institute of Adult Continuing Education (NIACE).

Westwood, J. (2003) 'The impact of adult education for mental health service users', *British Journal of Occupational Therapy*, **66** (11), 505–10.

Erikson's eight stages of normal human development

Age	Developmental stage	Key challenges	Characterisitcs
0–1	Infancy	Trust vs mistrust	Infants depend on parents for food and safety. If these are provided they learn to trust. If not, they learn to mistrust.
1–2	Toddler	Autonomy (independence) vs doubt (or shame)	Toddlers are starting to become independent. If this is encouraged and they receive reassurance for mistakes, they will develop autonomy. If parents are overprotective and disapproving, self-doubt develops.
2–6	Early childhood	Initiative vs guilt	Children have greater motor skills and can interact more. Encouragement but with appropriate discipline can help them become aware of their limits and channel their initiative into creative ideas. If not, they may feel guilt about taking initiative and shame about being creative.
6–12	Elementary and middle school years	Competence ('industry') vs inferiority	Children learn new skills and knowledge and learn to be productive members of society among their peers. Resolving these issues can make them confident and positive about success, learning and competence. If not, a sense of inferiority develops.
12–18	Adolescence	Identity vs role confusion	Adolescents ask themselves 'who am I?' This stage is about integrating all the previous stages and feeling confident in oneself. Failure to address this results in confusion, problems with decision making and choice in general as well as in finding a role in life.
19–40	Young adulthood	Intimacy vs isolation	Love relationships and development of intimacy is key at this stage. Positive development leads to the ability to form close relationships and share with others. Otherwise, there is isolation and a fear of commitment or being able to depend on others.
40–65	Middle adulthood	Generativity vs stagnation	This stage is about the ability to look outside oneself and at others, and to pass on knowledge to children. Problems here lead to self-centredness and stagnation.
65 to death	Late adulthood	Integrity vs despair	Older adults find integrity through an ability to reflect on their lives and their successes and failures. If there is a sense of fulfilment and achievement then there will be no fear of death. Otherwise there will be despair and a fear of death.

See also psychology.about.com/library/weekly/aa091500a.htm

Seven Adaptive Skills assessment checklist

(© N. Taylor and J. Chacksfield. Based on work by Anne Cronin Mosey)

Name: **Date:**   **Assessed by:**   **Observed activity:**

	Adaptive skill	✔	Sub-skills	Comments – add comments in the space below
1	Perceptual motor skill		Can remain balanced when moving	Useful for understanding physical responses in severely disabled individuals
			Can move both sides of the body appropriately and respond to sounds	
			Can perceive the body in the environment and use body parts appropriately	
			Can move in a coordinated way and understand sounds and language	
			Can tell the difference between right and left and remember sounds and words	
			Can use abstract ideas, can understand more complex language and give feedback	
2	Cognitive skill		Can use instinctive behaviour patterns to interact with the world	Useful for assessing ability to process information and identifying how best to present tasks
			Can make use of vision, touch, hearing and taste in a coordinated way	
			Can observe and remember interactions with the environment and put responses into sequence	
			Can set goals and act on these, can see people and things as separate from self, can imitate and learn from others	
			Can solve problems by trial and error and can watch and learn from observations	
			Can remember how experiences felt, can tell the difference between thought and action and know that everything needs a cause	
			Can name and classify objects, can hold a balanced view of all aspects of an object and understand the views of others	
			Can think flexibly, use logic and ideas or theories	
3	Drive-object skill		Can obtain satisfaction from people or things for short periods of time	NB The ability to tolerate a delay in satisfaction is important in this skill. This varies across all the sub-skills. These criteria are useful in understanding tolerance with an activity and ability to deal with frustration
			Can maintain satisfaction with one primary person or thing and continue this over time	
			Can express anger/frustration in a way that leads to satisfaction	
			Can transfer ability to obtain satisfaction from people or things other than the primary one	

	Adaptive skill	✔	Sub-skills	Comments – add comments in the space below
			Can create imaginary objects and can control anger/frustration	
			Can obtain results by using one object (recognising its strengths and limitations) or from a variety of objects	
4	**Dyadic interaction skill**		Can enter an association relationship (i.e. acquaintances)	Useful in assessing ability to relate to others
			Can interact in an authority relationship (accept training)	
			Can enter a friendship	
			Can enter peer-authority relationships (other learners can help)	
			Can enter an intimate relationship (close friend)	
			Can engage in nurturing relationships (supportive)	
5	**Group interaction skill**		Can participate in a parallel group (same room as others but limited interaction)	Useful in identifying the extent to which a person can participate in a group activity
			Can participate in a project group (shared task that is directed by trainer)	
			Can participate in an egocentric cooperative group (interacts and initiates activity in a group with trainer direction)	
			Can participate in a cooperative group (interacts and influences group to achieve goals with support from trainer)	
			Can participate in a mature group (self-directed group session)	
6	**Self-identity skill**		Can see self as a worthy object	Useful for assessing self-esteem, self-awareness and self-efficacy
			Knows own assets and limitations	
			Can see self as self-directed	
			Can see self as a productive, contributing member of society	
			Can see self in more depth	
			Can accept change associated with age	
7	**Sexual identity skill**		Can accept self as male or female	Useful for assessing if someone can cope with others they may be attracted to, challenging behaviour and lack of confidence about sexuality
			Accepts sexual maturation as positive	
			Can have a meaningful sexual relationship appropriately	
			Can maintain a sexual relationship	
			Can accept later-life sexual changes (e.g. menopause)	

Additional comments/action plan:

Safe and comfortable use of computer equipment

What can I do to help myself?

Make full use of the equipment provided, and adjust it to get the best from it and to avoid potential health problems. If your country's health and safety regulations apply to you, your employer should cover these things in training. It is worth setting up your workstation properly, to be as comfortable as possible.

Getting comfortable

- Adjust your chair and VDU to find the most comfortable position for your work. As a broad guide, your forearms should be approximately horizontal and your eyes the same height as the top of the VDU.
- Make sure you have enough work space to take whatever documents or other equipment you need.
- Try different arrangements of keyboard, screen, mouse and documents to find the best arrangement for you. A document holder may help you avoid awkward neck and eye movements.
- Arrange your desk and VDU to avoid glare, or bright reflections on the screen. This will be easiest if neither you nor the screen is directly facing windows or bright lights. Adjust curtains or blinds to prevent unwanted light.
- Make sure there is space under your desk to move your legs freely. Move any obstacles such as boxes or equipment.
- Avoid excess pressure from the edge of your seat on the backs of your legs and knees. A footrest may be helpful, particularly for smaller users.

Using the keyboard

- Adjust your keyboard to get a good typing position. A space in front of the keyboard is sometimes helpful for resting the hands and wrists when not typing.
- Try to keep your wrists straight when typing. Keep a soft touch on the keys and do not overstretch your fingers. Good keyboard technique is important.

Using a mouse

- Position the mouse within easy reach, so it can be used with the wrist straight. Sit upright and close to the desk, so you don't have to work with your mouse arm stretched. Move the keyboard out of the way if it is not being used.
- Support your forearm on the desk, and don't grip the mouse too tightly.
- Rest your fingers lightly on the buttons and do not press them hard.

Reading the screen

- Adjust the brightness and contrast controls on the screen to suit lighting conditions in the room.
- Make sure the screen surface is clean.
- In setting up software, choose options giving text that is large enough to read easily on your screen when you are sitting in a normal, comfortable working position. Select colours that are easy on the eye (avoid red text on a blue background or vice versa).
- Individual characters on the screen should be sharply focused and should not flicker or move. If they do, the VDU may need servicing or adjustment.

Posture and breaks

- Don't sit in the same position for long periods. Make sure you change your posture as often as practicable. Some movement is desirable, but avoid repeated stretching to reach things you need (if this happens a lot, rearrange your workstation).
- Most jobs provide opportunities to take a break from the screen, for example to do filing or photocopying. Make use of them. If there are no such natural breaks in your job, your employer should plan for you to have rest breaks. Frequent short breaks are better than fewer long ones.

(Adapted from the British Health and Safety Executive 2003 Working with VDUs advice leaflet, which is available online at www.hse.gov.uk/pubns/indg36.pdf.)

Section 2

Schemes of work

Session plans

Tutor notes

Schemes of work and Session plans

Introduction to Section 2

This section is for trainers and healthcare workers to help with the format of the group or sessions they will be taking.

The course has been split into three group categories. The first two groups have been prepared with limited availability of centre resources in mind, i.e. just a computer and whiteboard or flipchart. The third group is for centres with more extensive resources, such as the internet and software.

There are schemes of work and session plans for a 12-week term. All sessions are based on a two-hour time slot but they can be adjusted for one-hour sessions, or parts of the course can be used as required.

Tutor notes accompanying each session are also provided as guidance on how to teach the subject, and pointing out the benefits to learners and ways to adapt the subject to your learners' needs.

This printed book contains the first three sessions from each group, whereas the accompanying disk contains all 12 sessions in each of the three groups, along with all the resources needed for each session. Your own centre details can be added, if required, before making printouts from the disk.

The sessions from the various groups can be used separately or together depending on the ability of your learners. You can also easily adapt the resources if needed to suit your class.

About the three groups

Group 1

The first group of sessions is for learners who have very limited ability in motor skills and cognitive processing (for more details see page 9). These learners may need help with letter recognition and be encouraged by the structure of a regular learning routine. This group benefits from working as a group, identifying aspects of functioning in society and everyday life and learning basic computer operations such as formatting.

Group 2

The second group is for learners with the ability to work on their own and follow written instructions. This course is designed to concentrate on the effects of using various features and functions such as menus and icons.

Group 3

The third group is for those organisations that have internet access and are able to buy in software to aid with teaching.

Differentiation

This is a term used to describe the provisions you have made to cater for learners with either more or less ability than what is in your session plan. Although a class with everyone at the same stage would be ideal, it is very unlikely and you will have learners at differing levels.

The three groups can be interacted or resources can be adapted to help with learners at different levels of ability.

Computer adaptability

There are various ways to adapt the computer to make it easier for your learners to use effectively.

Adapting the mouse

Many users may struggle with the use of a mouse, possibly owing to a physical impairment or because the concept of looking at a screen instead of what the hand is doing is alien to them. This can be overcome in a number of ways by going to Start | Settings | Control Panel | Mouse, where the the following changes can be made:

- The mouse can be adapted for left hand users.
- The double-click speed can be adjusted for a faster or slower response.
- The ClickLock option can be turned on – this enables you to drag the mouse without needing to hold the button down (Windows XP only).
- The pointer can be enlarged.
- The colours can be changed for higher visibility.

Enlarging features

This can be done via Start | Settings | Control Panel | Display. On the Appearance tab you can change the font size to Large or Extra Large. You can also click on the Advanced tab in the Appearance dialog box to change the size of the window features, such as the title bar or message box.

From within an application such as Microsoft Word, you can:

- increase the Zoom size of the screen from the View menu
- choose the Normal view as opposed to the Print Layout view from the View menu
- choose double line spacing from the Format | Paragraph menu so text is easier to read.

Colour and high visibility

You can change the colour scheme of the computer by going to Start | Settings | Control Panel | Display, you can change the scheme to high contrast, large font sizes or customise the scheme to your personal preference.

Also, from within an application such as Microsoft Word, you can go to Tools | Options and on the General tab you can choose a blue background with white text.

The colour of the background can also be changed by going to Format | Background.

The cursor

The speed and thickness of the cursor can be adjusted from Start | Settings | Control Panel | Accessibility Options, on the Display tab.

Teaching tips

- **Follow the learner's pace**
  Some tutors expect their learners to be more advanced in their ICT skills at a certain stage than they may actually be (see page 9), especially if they are used to teaching mainstream classes. It is your job to help the learners proceed at whatever pace suits them, even if it feels as though you have been teaching the same thing for weeks. It is better to help them understand a few concepts confidently than bombard them with lots of skills that they are likely to forget. Helping learners to gain confidence is as much part of the teaching experience as helping them to gain new skills. The confidence will in turn help learners to want to learn more.

- **Don't take on the role of the nurses or key worker**
  You might find that some learners, being in a relaxed setting, may open up to you and wish to discuss any problems they have, medical or mental. Although you may feel comfortable listening to them you should make it clear that you cannot give medical advice (unless you are qualified to do so), and it would be better for them to let their key worker know any problems. This is better for the learner, and also for you, as you will not be aware of the full picture regarding your learner's health state and any advice you give could be damaging.

- **Personal safety**
  If you are working in a forensic setting, be aware of personal safety procedures (see page 23). It is usual for there to be another staff member in the room with you for safety reasons. Do not feel pressured to be in the room on your own with the learners while the other staff member 'pops out' for a minute or two if you do not feel comfortable. If you have any doubts or queries about your safety, raise these in your supervision meeting (see below).

- **Supervision and support**
  Supervision is not a case of someone looking over your shoulder seeing what you are doing. It is a chance for you as a tutor to off-load or bring to light any problems, worries, queries or successes you have encountered in your sessions. For more on supervision see page 23. With regard to support, if you feel you are 'out of your depth' or need extra help with accessing equipment or resources, ask for it. You have every right to. Your employer will want the best outcome for the learners as well, but as they are not in the session with you, they may not be aware of what is required.

- **Enjoy your session**
  You are working in a specialist area of teaching and the achievements and positive responses of your learners (no matter how small or how long it takes) are worth every input you have made.

Scheme of work for Group 1

Tutor name: **Course title:**

Day: **Time:**   **Location:**

Week	Session content	Resources
1 Introduction	• Find out about computer components • Mouse control skills	Building the computer exercise Computer components disk work Mouse control skills 1 and 2
2 Basic formatting	• More mouse control skills • Opening work • Saving work • Basic formatting	Sizes disk exercise Large icon cards Computer components matching exercise
3–12 Life topics	**These topics encourage group work and help learners think about the world around them, and their contributions and place within it.** **These sections consist of computer and written work, which build on mouse control skills, letter recognition and using keyboard skills. Extra help may be needed for character recognition by some learners when typing.**	
3 Jobs 4 Activities/hobbies 5 People/animals and where they live 6 Transport 7 Holidays 8 Signs and symbols 9 Families (Note: this may be a sensitive area for some learners – use discretion) 10 Countries and landmarks 11 Food and health 12 Weather and seasons	• Brief discussion with learners about the week's topic, how it relates to them, what they like/dislike/use • Learners type on the computer what they have discussed • Matching exercise • Filling in the letters exercise relating to topic on the computer • Keyboard skills • Discussion/typing about what can be done/used with the topic • Day's diary	Computers/laptops Matching exercises Word completion disk exercises Cut outs and pictures of day's topics that can facilitate discussions Flipchart/whiteboard Typing skills worksheets Large icon cards Picture/word search

Group 1 Session plans

Course: **Date:**

Session number: 1 of 12   **Tutor:**

Aims:
- for learners to use the mouse confidently
- to know the common parts of the computer.

Objectives:
To introduce the way a mouse works and how to move it. To show the parts which make up a computer, and to recognise them by name.

Differentiation:

Time (mins)	Session content	Learning activity	Resources
Section 1 10–15	• Welcome learners, introductions • Ask what prior experience they have had and what they would like to learn • Explain what they will be doing on the course • If not known prior to session, find out special learner requirements to enhance their learning	**Learner:** Group discussion, Group identity forming, Listening **Tutor:** Find out about learners in the group and their specific requirements	Relevant paperwork according to centre requirements Notebook for tutor to detail learners' requirements
Section 2 20	• Look at the parts of the computer that are in front of them – monitor, keyboard, mouse, unit, printer • Elicit names from learners of the parts of the computer they recognise, explaining what each part is for • Followed by 'Building the computer' exercise in pairs	**Learners:** Group work Pair work Reinforcing information **Tutor:** Encouraging learner to express information they already know Q&A	Whiteboard/flipchart Pens Building the computer exercise Scissors
Section 3 15	• Look at the features of the mouse – shape, buttons • Show/help learners hold and move the mouse left, right, up and down • Explain stages to log on the computer to get to the desktop – *help may be needed for passwords and using the mouse*	**Learners:** Listening skills Individual practice using the computer **Tutor:** Explanation with practical for visual and auditory learning	Whiteboard/flipchart Pens How to turn on the computer handout for reference
10	Break		
Section 4 20	• Instructions with demonstration for mouse control skills exercises	**Learners:** Individual or group work following demonstrations **Tutor:** Explanation with practical for visual and auditory learning	Mouse control skills 1 Mouse control skills 2
Section 5 20	• Verbal recap on computer components, eliciting answers from learners • Print work	**Learners:** Group work **Tutor:** Assessing learners' knowledge	The computer system disk exercise Printer

Time (mins)	Session content	Learning activity	Resources
Section 6 10	• Brief discussion with learners about what they had learnt in the session and how they felt about it, encouraging them to recap earlier events • Learners type out weekly diary of the session's events using the computer • Print work	**Learners:** Group discussion to recall information **Tutor:** Encouraging, starting group discussion/Q&A session	Whiteboard/flipchart Pens Printer
Section 7 5	• Make sure learners have printed their work • Show learners how to shut down the computer	**Learners:** Listening to instructions **Tutor:** Instructions with demonstration	

Notes/comments/evaluation:

Course: **Date:**

Session number: 2 of 12 **Tutor:**

Aims:
- for learners to use the mouse confidently
- to know the common parts of the computer.

Objectives:
Highlighting techniques, basic formatting skills, opening/saving work using the floppy disk.

Differentiation:

Time (mins)	Session content	Learning activity	Resources
Section 1 15	• Recap last session with discussion – what they have done and how they have done it • Matching components to name exercise	**Learners:** Group discussion to recall information Pair work for exercise **Tutor:** Encouraging, starting group discussion/Q&A session	Computer components matching exercise Scissors
Section 2 15–20	Basic formatting: • Show how get a blank page using the toolbar • Learners type their name with the date underneath – *show how to move the cursor down with the enter key* • Show learners how to highlight their name and change the size with the size icon • Learners then change the size of the date • Sizes disk exercise	**Learners:** Listening to instructions as a group Following visual aids Individual practice on the computer **Tutor:** Instructions with demonstration	New Page and Font Size large icon cards Changing the size disk work
Section 3 15	• Show how to get a blank page again • Learners type the **Day** with **Computer session** underneath • Learners change the size of the **day** then change the colour using the toolbar • Learners then change size of **computer session**, then the colour using the toolbar • Colour disk exercise	**Learners:** Listening to instructions as a group Following visual aids Individual practice on the computer **Tutor:** Instructions with demonstration	New Page, Font Size and Font Colour large icon cards Changing the colour disk work
10	Break		
Section 4 15–20	Instructions with demonstration for saving work: • Open a new page and type **saving work** • Click on the save button on the toolbar • Explain the Save in and the File name boxes of the Save as dialog box • Change the Save in box to 3½ Floppy (A:) • Add a File name and click Save, before closing the work • Save the 2 pieces of earlier work using above methods • Close Microsoft Word	**Learners:** Listening to instructions as a group Following visual diagrams Individual practice on the computer **Tutor:** Instructions with demonstration	Whiteboard/flipchart with step-by-step instructions Save large icon card
Section 5 5	• Recap with enlarged toolbar icons, the icons learnt earlier i.e. sizes, colours, new page, save	**Learners:** Group work to encourage recalling information **Tutor:** Encourage group interaction	New Page, Font Size and Font Colour and Save large icon cards

Time (mins)	Session content	Learning activity	Resources
Section 6 10–15	Instructions with demonstration for opening work: • Open Microsoft Word • Click the Open icon on the toolbar with the aid of the Open enlarged icon picture • Explain the Look in: section • Change the Look in box to 3¹/₂ Floppy (A:) (or whichever disk you are using) • Click the first file that you need • Open the 2 pieces of work from earlier using above methods • Close Microsoft Word	**Learners:** Listening to instructions as a group Following visual diagrams Individual practice on the computer **Tutor:** Instructions with demonstration	Whiteboard/flipchart with written step-by-step instructions Open large icon card
Section 7 5	• Recap with large icon cards • Learners each have a picture of the enlarged icons. Tutor asks which picture is for which function and learner holds up the correct picture	**Learners:** Group/team work to encourage recalling information **Tutor:** Encourage group interaction	Large icon cards
Section 8 10–15	• Brief discussion with learners about what they had learnt in the session and how they felt about it, encouraging learners to recap earlier events • Learners type out weekly diary of the session's events using the computer • Print work	**Learners:** Group discussion to recall information **Tutor:** Encouraging, starting group discussion/Q&A session	Whiteboard/flipchart Pens Printer
5	• Show learners how to shut down the computer • Make sure learners have printed their work	**Learners:** Listening to instructions **Tutor:** Instructions with demonstration	

Notes/comments/evaluation:

Course: **Date:**

Session number: 3 of 12   **Tutor:**

Aims:
- for learners to use the mouse confidently
- interact within a group and be able to share experiences.

Objectives:
To recognise with visual and written aids different job types and the people/equipment associated with them.

Differentiation:

Time (mins)	Session content	Learning activity	Resources
Section 1 15	• Recap last session with discussion – what they have done and how they did it. • Open icons exercise for open practice • Fill in the correct icon name then save when finished for saving practice	**Learners:** Group discussion to recall information Group/individual work for exercise **Tutor:** Encouraging/starting group discussion/Q&A session	Icons exercise
Section 2 15–20	• Talk with learners about job types what sort of jobs they do/would like to do or know that someone does and then type about it. • Matching jobs and equipment exercise on paper	**Learners:** Group discussion Recognising jobs and the tools needed **Tutor:** Encouraging/starting group discussion	Whiteboard/flipchart Pens Biros/pencils for learners Matching jobs and places exercise
Section 3 15	• Filling in letters exercise on the computer of different jobs and places of work	**Learners:** Group/individual work to strengthen mouse skills and reiterate job types **Tutor:** Encouraging group interaction Visual assessment	Jobs word completion disk work
10	Break		
Section 4 15	• Typing skills practice to help learners search and recognise letters on the keyboard • Change size of first 5 words • Change colour of last 5 words • Save and print work	**Learners:** Individual work to encourage key recognition Recap on formatting **Tutor:** Encourage typing independence Visual assessment	Jobs typing skills worksheet Font Colour and Font Size large icon cards Printer
Section 5 15–20	• Discussion about a particular job elicited from learners – what people need for that job and the order things are done in. Write points on board • Learners type up results on the computer • Format title so it is bigger and a different colour than the rest of the text • Save and print work	**Learners:** Group discussion Recognising jobs and the tools needed **Tutor:** Elicit learner knowledge	Whiteboard/flipchart Pens Printer Font Colour and Font Size large icon cards
Section 6 10	• Picture search on paper	**Learners:** Individual/pair work to find various pictures	Jobs picture search

Time (mins)	Session content	Learning activity	Resources
Section 7 10–15	• Brief discussion with learners about what they had learnt in the session and how they felt about it, encouraging learners to recap earlier events • Learners type out weekly diary of the session's events using the computer • Print work	**Learners:** Group discussion/reflection **Tutor:** Group discussion, Q&A	Whiteboard/flipchart Pens Printer
	• Show learners how to shut down the computer • Make sure learners have printed their work	**Learners:** Listening to instructions **Tutor:** Instructions with demonstration	

Notes/comments/evaluation:

Scheme of work for Group 2

Tutor name: **Course title:**

Day: **Time:**   **Location:**

Week	Session content	Resources
1	• Looking at computer components • Introducing basic formatting • Using the undo button	Computer components handout How to . . . handouts Word processing checklist Large icon cards
2	• Inserting and deleting	Components recap disk work Large icon cards Inserting and deleting disk work and worksheets Practice worksheets
3	• Alignments • Adding text colour • Creating adverts	Alignments disk work and large icon cards Matching icons worksheet Flyer/adverts examples
4	• Using cut/copy and paste • Changing line spacing	Basic formatting worksheet How to . . . handouts Computer skills crossword Line spacing work
5	• Page setup features • Find and replace function	Spellcheck disk work Page setup practice Find and replace disk work What goes where disk work
6	• Recap exercises	Recap worksheets
7	• Adding pictures • Resizing pictures • Moving pictures	How to add graphics handouts Pictures to insert from disk
8	• Adding WordArt • Adding page borders	Matching icons 2 How to . . . handouts
9	• Using AutoShapes to draw pictures • Adding colours to AutoShapes • Using Paint	How to use AutoShapes handouts
10	• Letter typing skills • Inserting symbols • Bullets and numbering	Letters worksheet Letters handout Bullets and numbering disk work How to add bullets and numbering handout
11	• Introducing tables	Creating tables handouts Merging cells disk work
12	• Course recap	Recap skills quiz Feedback, evaluation forms Certificates

Group 2 Session plans

Course: **Date:**

Session number: 1 of 12   **Tutor:**

Aims:
- recognise computer components by name
- use the bold, italics, underline, font style, font size and undo button from the toolbar.

Objectives:
By the end of the session, learners will be able to identify basic computer components and use the undo button.

Differentiation:

Time (mins)	Session content	Learning activity	Resources
Section 1 15	• Welcome learners, introductions • Ask what prior experience they have had and what they would like to learn. • Explain about what they will be doing on the course. • If not known prior to session, find out special learner requirements to enhance their learning	**Learners:** Group discussion Group identity-forming Listening **Tutor:** Find out about learners in the group and their specific requirements	Relevant paperwork according to centre requirements Notebook for tutor to detail learners' requirements
Section 2 10	• Look at the parts of the computer that are in front of them -- monitor, keyboard, mouse, unit, printer • Elicit names from learners of the parts of the computer they recognise, explaining what each part is for	**Learners:** Group work Reinforcing information **Tutor:** Encouraging learners to express information they already know Q&A	Whiteboard/flipchart Pens Computer components handout
Section 3 10	• Explain, with practice, the stages to log on the computer to get to the desktop -- *passwords should be written down beforehand* • Practice logging on and shutting down	**Learners:** Listening skills Individual practice using the computer **Tutor:** Explanation with practical for visual and auditory learning	Whiteboard/flipchart Pens How to turn on the computer handout
Section 4 20	• Explain about the use of MS Word – what it can be used for, how we are going to use it in the course • Show learners how to log on to MS Word – demonstration with practice • Look at the MS Word screen, introduce the title bar, menu bar, toolbars, icons, insertion point, scroll bars, minimise, restore and close buttons • Demonstrate, with learner practice, how to display/remove toolbars, and how to minimise, restore and close windows • Windows basics exercise	**Learners:** Listening skills, group and individual work to learn new computer skills **Tutor:** Facilitating learning with modelling techniques, followed by visual assessment of exercise	How to log on to MS Word handout The MS Word 2000 screen handout Windows basics exercise
10		Break	

Time (mins)	Session content	Learning activity	Resources
Section 5 10	• Verbal recap on computer components with pictures • In pairs, learners complete the Blank MS Word screen disk work	**Learners:** Group and pair work for reinforcement of previous skills **Tutor:** Q&A session with computer components to assess learner knowledge	Computer components picture cards Blank MS Word screen disk work
Section 6 25	• Introduce the Word processing checklist and how to use it • Introduce basic typing skills and keyboard keys (backspace key, return key, etc.), starting with name. Show how to use the undo button for mistakes • Demonstration with practice for highlighting techniques, explain why it is needed, followed by changing font size and font style demonstrations • Changing size and styles exercise	**Learners:** Listening skills Group and individual work to learn new computer skills **Tutor:** Facilitating learning with modelling techniques, followed by assessment of exercise	Word processing checklist How to highlight text handout Undo button, Font Style and Font Size large icon cards Change the size and style exercise
Section 7 10	• Bold, italic and underline from the toolbar demonstrations, followed by BIU disk work	**Learners:** Listening skills Individual practice using the computer **Tutor:** Explanation with practical for visual and auditory learning	Bold, Italic and Underline large icon card BIU disk work
	• Day's recap and shut down	**Learners:** Discussion, questions and feedback about the session **Tutor:** Discussion and questions about what was learnt in the session	

Notes/comments/evaluation:

Course: **Date:**

Session number: 2 of 12   **Tutor:**

Aims:
* recognise computer components by name
* use the bold, italics, underline, font style, font size and undo button from the toolbar
* insert and delete text
* open and save work.

Objectives:
By the end of the session, learners will be able to identify and use the bold, italics and underline buttons, and change the font size and style independently.

Differentiation:

Time (mins)	Session content	Learning activity	Resources
Section 1 15–20	• Recap computer components on the screen with Components recap disk work • Verbal recap with large icon cards for undo button, font style and size, bold, italics and underline, followed by Word basics disk work • Learners fill in familiar icons with icons handout sheet	**Learners:** Learners will work individually to recap previous skills learnt, followed by group work **Tutor:** Visual assessment	Components recap disk work Bold, Italic and Underline, Undo, Font Size and Font Style large icon cards Word basics disk work Icons handout
Section 2 20	• Explanation of how to insert text – learners type a sentence, e.g. 'Today I am at [centre name]', and then insert the word 'learning' after the word 'am' • Practice with a second sentence • 'The sun is hot' – insert the word 'sometimes' after the word 'is' – followed by Inserting 1 disk work	**Learners:** Listening skills Individual practice using the computer **Tutor:** Explanation with practical for visual and auditory learning	Inserting 1 disk work and worksheet
Section 3 15	• Explanation of how to delete text from the sentence typed earlier – 'Today I am learning at [centre name]' – delete the word 'learning' after the word 'am' • Practice with the second sentence – 'The sun is sometimes hot' – delete the word 'sometimes' after the word 'is', followed by Deleting 1 disk work	**Learners:** Listening skills Individual practice using the computer **Tutor:** Explanation with practical for visual and auditory learning	Deleting 1 disk work and worksheet
10	Break		
Section 4 15	• Explanation with demonstration to show how to save a document using File I Save As • Learners practise creating a new document with the new page icon on the toolbar and saving the document, first with their name, then saving a new document with the date	**Learners:** Listening skills Individual practice using the computer **Tutor:** Explanation with practical for visual and auditory learning	New Page large icon card Saving a document handout

Time (mins)	Session content	Learning activity	Resources
Section 5 10	• Explanation with demonstration to show how to open a document using the toolbar. Learners practise opening the work saved earlier, followed by verbal recap of the procedure on how to save a document and how to open a document	**Learners:** Listening skills Individual practice using the computer **Tutor:** Explanation with practical for visual and auditory learning	Opening a document handout
Section 6 20	• Learners practise opening and saving the inserting and deleting work with disk exercises	**Learners:** Individual practice of day's skills **Tutor:** Individual encouragement Visual assessment	Session 2 worksheet About me disk work About my lesson disk work
	• Day's recap and shut down	**Learners:** Discussion, questions and feedback about the session **Tutor:** Discussion and questions about what was learnt in the session	

Notes/comments/evaluation:

Course: **Date:**

Session number: 3 of 12   **Tutor:**

Aims:
*   to insert and delete text
*   to open and save work
*   to add colour to text
*   to use the correct alignment for text.

Objectives:
By the end of the session, learners will be able to create an advert using the formatting skills learnt.

Differentiation:

Time (mins)	Session content	Learning activity	Resources
Section 1 15–20	• Recap last session, followed by verbal instructions elicited from learners on how to insert and delete • Inserting 2 and Deleting 2 disk work • Recap New Page and Open icons with large icon cards – learners fill in checklist if needed	**Learners:** Group discussion followed by individual practice **Tutor:** Q&A to help reinforce skills learnt Assessment of previous session's knowledge	Inserting 2 disk work Deleting 2 disk work New Page and Open large icon cards
Section 2 15	• Explanation of what the alignment buttons do and where they are on the toolbar • Practise using alignments with name on a new page followed by alignment practice encouraging learners to remember how to open work	**Learners:** Listening skills Individual practice using the computer **Tutor:** Explanation with practical for visual and auditory learning	Alignment large icon card Alignments example sheet Alignment practice disk work
Section 3 15	• Explanation of how to change the text colour and when you may want to, showing where it is on the toolbar • Practise changing the text colour with name on a new page followed by colours and alignment practice, encouraging learners to remember how to open work	**Learners:** Listening skills Individual practice using the computer **Tutor:** Explanation with practical for visual and auditory learning	Font Colour large icon card Colour and alignment practice disk work
10	Break		
Section 4 10–15	• In pairs or individually, learners complete the Matching the icons 1 worksheet on paper followed by discussion about any problems or queries they may have on using icons, inserting and deleting and opening and saving work	**Learners:** Individual or pair work followed by group discussion **Tutor:** Q&A to help reinforce skills learnt Assessment of knowledge	Matching the icons 1 worksheet
Section 5 30–35	• Learners complete an advert/flyer/invitation using the basic formatting skills they have learnt to date	**Learners:** Individual practice of days skills **Tutor:** Individual encouragement Visual assessment	Adverts example sheet Flyer/Invitation examples

Time (mins)	Session content	Learning activity	Resources
	• Day's recap and shut down	**Learners:** Discussion, questions and feedback about the session **Tutor:** Discussion and questions about what was learnt in the session	

Notes/comments/evaluation:

Scheme of work for Group 3

Tutor name: **Course title:**

Day: **Time:**   **Location:**

Week	Session content	Resources
1	• Initial assessment and introduction to the computer	SEMERC Assessability software Mouse control skills disk work Components handouts
2	• Initial assessment (continued)	SEMERC Assessability software Typing skills program Components disk work and worksheets
3	• Using the internet introduction	Internet connection Typing skills program Internet basics handouts
4	• Searching for information on the internet • General signs and symbols	Internet connection SEMERC Signs and Symbols software How to search for information handout Quiz
5	• Travel signs and symbols • Searching for holidays on the internet	Internet connection SEMERC Signs and Symbols software Travel signs Travel pictures exercise
6	• Independent web browsing	Internet connection List of various web sites Read&Write Gold software Typing skills program
7	• Developing listening and observation skills with hazards around the home	My Home passage Texthelp software SEMERC Out and About 2 software Hazards worksheet
8	• Developing listening and observation skills with hazards outside	My Area passage Texthelp software SEMERC Out and About 2 software Hazards worksheet
9	• Developing listening and recalling information skills with hazards and activities	My Activities passage Texthelp software SEMERC Out and About 1 software Hazards worksheet
10	• Developing listening and recalling information skills with hazards and jobs	My Job passage Texthelp software SEMERC Out and About 1 software Hazards worksheet
11	• Skills for in and around the home	SEMERC Out and About 2 software Internet connection
12	• Course recap	

Group 3 Session plans

Course: **Date:**

Session number: 1 of 12   **Tutor:**

Aims:
- to determine learners' assessment levels
- for learners to identify the common parts of the computer by name.

Objectives.
By the end of the session, learners will be able to identify basic computer components and have completed three sections of the basic skills assessment.

Differentiation:

Time (mins)	Session content	Learning activity	Resources
Section 1 15	• Welcome learners, introductions • Ask what prior experience they have had and what they would like to learn • Explain about what they will be doing on the course • If not known prior to the session, find out special learner requirements to enhance their learning	**Learners:** Group discussion Group identity forming Listening **Tutor:** Find out about learners in the group and their specific requirements	Relevant paperwork according to centre requirements Notebook for tutor to detail learners' requirements
Section 2 10	• Look at the parts of the computer that are in front of them – monitor, keyboard, mouse, unit, printer • Elicit names from learners of the parts of the computer they recognise, explaining what each part is for	**Learners:** Group work Reinforcing information **Tutor:** Encouraging learners to express information they already know Q&A	Whiteboard/flipchart Pens Computer components handout
Section 3 10	• Explain the stages to log on to the computer to get to the desktop -- *passwords should be written down beforehand* • Practise logging on and shutting down	**Learners:** Listening skills Individual practice using the computer **Tutor:** Explanation with practical for visual and auditory learning	Whiteboard/flipchart Pens How to turn on the computer handout
10	Break		
Section 4 20	• Instructions with demonstration using the mouse with disk	**Learners:** Following demonstrations from tutor to actively move and click the mouse **Tutor:** Explanation with practical for visual and auditory learning	Mouse control skills 1 Mouse control skills 2
Section 5 45	• Load SEMERC Assessability software • Learners type in their personal details and continue on to the first section • Discussion with the class about how they find using the disk • Learners carry on with the next two sections	**Learners:** Entry-level basic skills assessment using auditory, cognitive and visual abilities **Tutor:** Assessing learner knowledge	SEMERC Assessability software

Time (mins)	Session content	Learning activity	Resources
	• Day's recap and shut down	**Learners:** Discussion, questions and feedback about the session **Tutor:** Discussion and questions about what was learnt in the session	

Notes/comments/evaluation:

Course: **Date:**

Session number: 2 of 12 **Tutor:**

Aims:
- to determine learners' assessment levels
- for learners to identify the common parts of the computer by name.

Objectives:
By the end of the session, learners will have finished the basic skills assessment.

Differentiation:

Time (mins)	Session content	Learning activity	Resources
Section 1 10	• Recap how to log on to the computer • Recap computer components on the screen with Components recap disk work	**Learners:** Learners will work individually to recap previous skills learnt **Tutor:** Visual assessment	Components recap disk work
Section 2 30	• Load SEMERC Assessability software • Complete the logical and jigsaw part of the assessment	**Learners:** Entry-level basic skills assessment using auditory, cognitive and visual abilities **Tutor:** Assessing learner knowledge	SEMERC Assessability software
Section 3 15	• Learners complete a jigsaw of computer components • Learners put in order the how to log on instructions	**Learners:** Individual or pair work to put items in order **Tutor:** Assessing learner knowledge	Computer components jigsaw How to turn on the computer cut out sheet Scissors
10	Break		
Section 4 15	• Complete the rest of the assessment and print results	**Learners:** Entry-level basic skills assessment using auditory, cognitive and visual abilities **Tutor:** Assessing learner knowledge	SEMERC Assessability software
Section 5 15	• Typing skills practice	**Learners:** Individual practice to using keyboard **Tutor:** Visual assessment of keyboard skills	Typing skills program
	• Day's recap and shut down	**Learners:** Discussion, questions and feedback about the session **Tutor:** Discussion and questions about what was learnt in the session	

Notes/comments/evaluation:

Course: **Date:**

Session number: 3 of 12   **Tutor:**

Aims:
- learners to log on to the internet
- add a web address in the address bar
- look at a different page using links
- search for information on the web.

Objectives:
By the end of the session, learners will know where to type a web address and how to follow a link.

Differentiation:

Time (mins)	Session content	Learning activity	Resources
Section 1 20	• Explain what the web is and what it is used for • Demonstration on how to log on to the internet • Brief look at features of the internet browser, followed by typing in web addresses	**Learners:** Listening skills Individual practice using the internet **Tutor:** Explanation with practical for visual and auditory learning	Internet connection How to log on to the internet handout Internet Explorer web browser handout Web addresses worksheet
Section 2 20	• Look at links and how they are used, followed by using links exercise	**Learners:** Listening skills Individual practice using the internet **Tutor:** Explanation with practical for visual and auditory learning	Internet connection Using links exercise
Section 3 10	• Internet basics quiz on the computer	**Learners:** Individual or pair work **Tutor:** Assessing learner knowledge	Internet basics quiz
10	Break		
Section 4 35–40	• Learners can use this time to search for places and items of interest, e.g. local services, banks, local college courses or what is happening locally this month in their area • Encourage learners to write down or print out what they have found out	**Learners:** Listening skills Individual practice using the internet **Tutor:** Encourage learners to use links and collect information Visual assessment	Internet connection Whiteboard/flipchart
Section 5 5–10	• Typing skills practice	**Learners:** Individual practice in using keyboard **Tutor:** Visual assessment of keyboard skills	Typing skills program
	• Day's recap and shut down	**Learners:** Discussion, questions and feedback about the session **Tutor:** Discussion and questions about what was learnt in the session	

Notes/comments/evaluation:

Tutor notes

Every effort has been made to ensure that the session plans and resources are as easy to use as possible, but it is important to familiarise yourself with the required resources for each section as some need to be transferred to a disk for the learners to use, some are worksheets that learners will give back to you at the end of the session and some are handouts for learners to keep.

The resources have been designed so that learners can alternate between the computer and paper-based work. This helps to provide variety with the topics and minimise the effects of tiredness on the eyes when looking at the screen for too long. It also gives learners the chance to benefit from a variety of resources, showing strengths in areas that may not necessarily be computer based, for example memory or searching skills, which in turn gives them confidence to contribute to other parts of the session they may not have tried before.

When working with the resources designed for Group 1, the paper-based worksheets encourage reflection and contributions from learners on the topic for that session as well as discussion and group work. It is also a bit of fun!

A sans serif font (fonts without twirly bits on the letters) is used in most of the exercises as it is similar to that on the keyboard for easy letter recognition.

For typing skills, there is an upper case as well as a lower case (but with initial capital) worksheet, to cater for those learners that can distinguish between upper and lower case letters.

When using the worksheets and handouts, it might be worth finding out what colour paper your learners prefer to use as some colour schemes, for example black print on yellow paper, are better for learners with visual impairments.

Keep the composition of your group in mind, as you may want to adapt some resources to reflect the group that you are teaching, for example by using cultural holidays.

The illustrated Tutor notes from the first three sessions of the three groups are presented on the following pages. A complete set of Tutor notes, in this case without the graphics resources interspersed, is on the accompanying CD. The resources themselves are also all on the CD, with the group, session and section referenced in the top right-hand corner of each page.

Tutor notes: Group 1/Session 1

Section 1

This is where you find out about your learners' requirements and fill in paperwork such as Individual Learning Plans/Target settings for the learners, and find out their knowledge of computers and what they have done before. This helps to see whether they are suitable for your session or whether another course would be more beneficial to them.

The aim of group forming is so that learners feel more comfortable to participate in the session among their peers.

The help of a support worker may be needed to help you with the group.

Section 2

Resources: Building the computer exercise

This is to help learners recognise the various computer components and what they do. Encourage the learners to say what they already know (eliciting information), for example many may know what a keyboard is for, as this will give them confidence. The Building the computer exercise can be done individually, in pairs or in a group, depending on your group situation. To use the exercise, cut out the individual parts of the computer for learners to put in the right order.

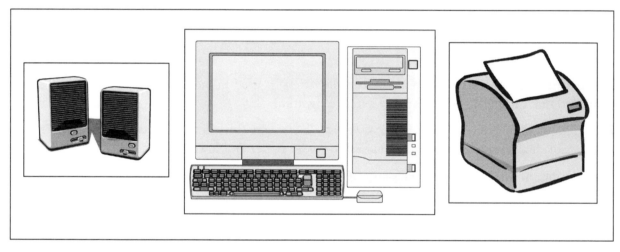

Building the computer exercise

Section 3

Resources: How to turn on the computer handout

Some learners may have never used a mouse before or may find it difficult owing to a medical condition or a disability, and you will need to be aware of this. It can take some learners longer than others to get used to using the mouse and identifying the correct button to use when selecting icons or buttons on the screen.

To log on, make sure you know your centre's setup, such as passwords. An explanation of the desktop would be needed so that learners know what they are aiming for.

Section 4

Resources: Mouse control skills 1 and 2

To use the mouse exercises, ask the questions on the question sheet for learners to click into and type the answers in the correct coloured box/arrow.

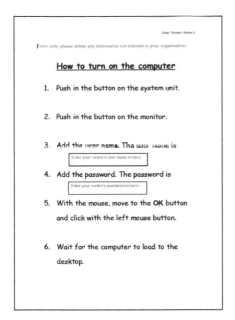

How to turn on the computer handout

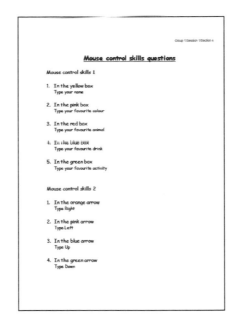

Mouse control skills questions

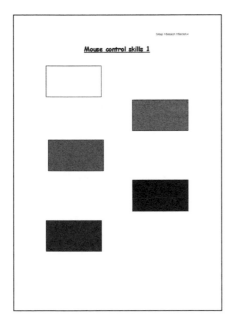

Mouse control skills 1 disk work

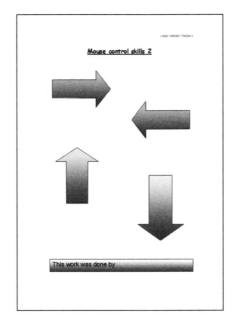

Mouse control skills 2 disk work

Section 5

Resources: The computer system disk exercise

Brief recap with learners on computer components to help reinforce information learnt in Section 2. To use, learners fill in the names of the computer parts after clicking in the space provided.

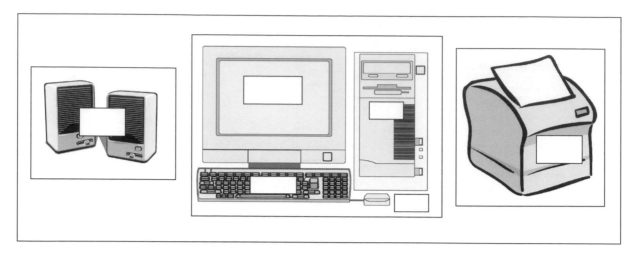

The computer system disk exercise

Section 6

Consolidation of skills learnt. Points can be written on the whiteboard or flipchart for learners to be able to type the information on the computer in their weekly diary. The diary can be just a few lines or more if learners are capable, with the computer class as the title (or something similar) and the date. This is a way for learners and trainers to have evidence of what they have learnt in that session.

Tutor notes: Group 1/Session 2

Section 1

Resources: Computer components matching exercise; Scissors

Recap with learners on what they had done in the previous session. This helps assess the knowledge of the learners and follow on to the new session. Any learners who were not in the previous session will also benefit from the recap

To use the exercise, either cut out the names so that they can be linked to the correct picture, or learners can write the correct name above the picture. Both or either worksheet can be used.

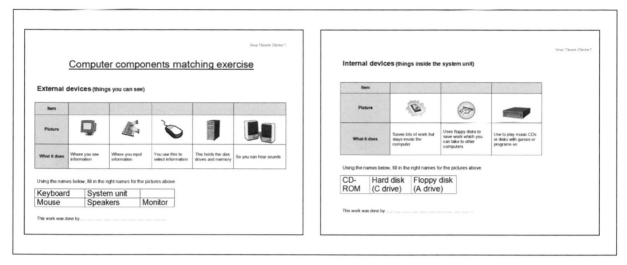

Computer components matching exercise

Section 2

Resources: New Page and Font Size large icon cards; Changing the size disk work

You will be introducing the use of some of the toolbar buttons. These buttons can be enlarged by going to Tools on the menu bar, then Customize. On the dialog box that opens, click on the Options tab and then tick the box next to Large Icons. This, however, does not change the size of the Font Style or Font Size boxes so help may be needed for those who find the buttons too small to select properly.

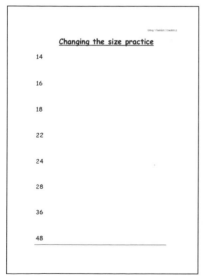

Changing the size disk work

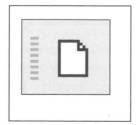

New Page large icon

Font Size large icon

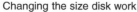

Section 3

Resources: New Page, Font Size and Font Colour icon cards; Changing the colour disk work

Toolbar buttons can be enlarged on the screen, as mentioned above (Section 2). Use the large icon cards when you are referring to a particular button as a visual aid to help with remembering what that button looks like.

Changing the colour disk work

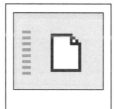

New Page large icon card

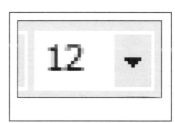

Font size large icon card

Font colour large icon card

Section 5

Resources: New Page, Font Size, Font Colour and Save large icon cards

Hold up the large icon cards one at a time for learners to say what button it is.

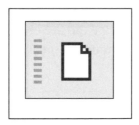

New Page large icon card

Font size large icon card

Font colour large icon card

Save large icon card

Section 6

Resources: Open large icon card

Use the Open icon on the toolbar as opposed to the File menu and Open. Give a brief overview of the Open dialog box, concentrating on making sure they have the right drive/folder in the Look In: section, for example $3^{1}/_{2}$ Floppy or My Documents. This may take some time for learners to get used to; this section is more of an introduction. Learners will become more familiar with the process as they go through the course, as they will be opening much of the disk work they will need.

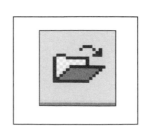

Open large icon card

Section 7

Resources: New Page, Font Size, Font Colour and Open large icon cards

This can be done in a speed form, with learners racing against each other or as all learners selecting the correct card.

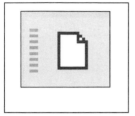

New Page large icon card

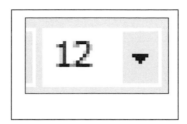

Font size large icon card

Font colour large icon card

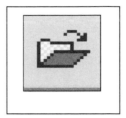

Open large icon card

Section 8

Consolidation of skills learnt. Points can be written on the whiteboard or flipchart for learners to be able to type the information on the computer in their weekly diary. The diary can be just a few lines or more if learners are capable, with the computer class as the title (or something similar) and the date. This is a way for learners and trainers to have evidence of what they have learnt in that session.

Tutor notes: Group 1/Session 3

Section 1

Resources: Icons exercise

When opening and saving the exercise, relay the points on how to open and save a document.

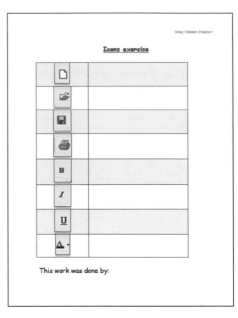

Icons exercise

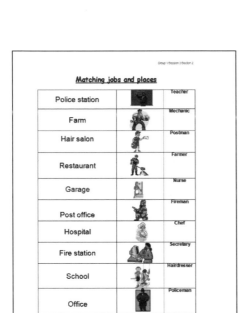

Matching jobs and places exercise

Section 2

Resources: Matching jobs and places exercise

Encourage the learners to draw from experience when talking about job types.

To use the exercise, either draw a line between matching items, or numbers/letters next to each item could be used to identify matching items.

Section 3

Resources: Jobs word completion disk work

Give clues as to the type of job listed, for example tools needed or where you would see this person, and encourage the learners to guess. You may need to help some learners find the keys on the keyboard. To move to the next box to input the letters, learners can use either the mouse or the tab key.

You may also want to make sure the Caps Lock key is on so the letters all look the same for those learners using the upper case exercise.

Answers: 1. Policeman; 2. Dentist; 3. Gardener; 4.Firewoman; 5. Zookeeper; 6. Nurse; 7. Soldier; 8. Waiter; 9. Actor; 10. Doctor

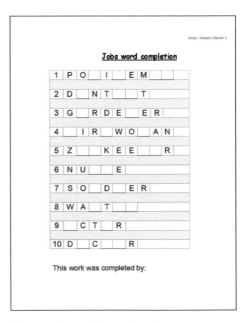

Jobs word completion disk work

Section 4

Resources: Jobs typing skills worksheet; Font Colour and Font Size large icon cards

The typing skills worksheets are to help learners find letters on the keyboard. Two or three of the same letter are used for neighbouring words on the worksheet, for example On and One.

Over time they will be able to find the letters more quickly. The words can then be used to practise formatting skills.

Jobs typing skills
(Upper case)

1	POLICE
2	POLICING
3	ZOOKEEPER
4	ZOOLOGIST
5	OFFICE WORKER
6	FARMER
7	FARMYARD
8	TEACHER
9	TRAFFIC WARDEN
10	TYPIST
11	BUILDER
12	BRICKLAYER

Jobs typing skills practice

Section 5

Resources: Font Colour and Font Size large icon cards

Talk about a particular job, for example a policeman, and discuss the type of training which may be needed, what they do in the job and the good and bad points of the job. This promotes independent thinking.

Font colour large icon card

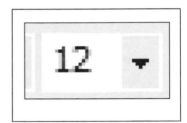

Font size large icon card

Section 6

Resources: Jobs picture search

This is an activity that can be completed individually, in pairs or in groups. It is like a word search, but learners are finding pictures instead of words.

It is easier for some learners to identify an image as opposed to a series of letters.

Jobs picture search

Tutor notes: Group 2/Session 1

Section 1

This is so you can find out more about your learners' needs and requirements. You may have to adapt some of the resources according to the learners' needs. Explaining what you are planning for the course is an indication for learners to see if the course is right for them.

Section 2

Resources: **Computer components handout**

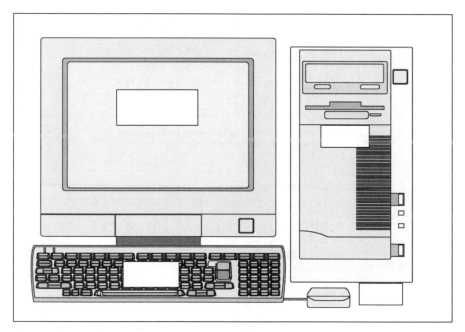

Computer components handout

Section 3

Resources: **How to turn on the computer handout**

Group 2/Session 1/Section 3

How to turn on the computer

1. Click the button on the system unit

2. Click the button on the monitor

3. Your screen may request you to put in a username and password – wait for it to load to the username and password screen

4. Type in your username and password

Username	
Password	

5. When you have typed in your username and password, click the OK button

6. Wait for your computer to load to the desktop.

How to turn on the computer handout

Section 4

Resources: How to log on to MS Word handout; The MS Word screen handout; Windows basics exercise

Showing the parts of the screen familiarises the features. The icons do not need to be identified individually at this stage as the students will get to know them later on in the course.

Possible uses for MS Word could be reports, adverts, flyers, cards, stories and letters.

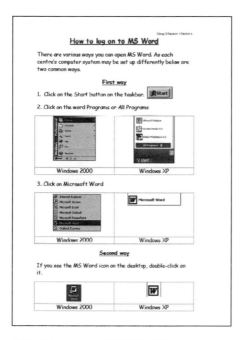

How to log on to MS Word handout

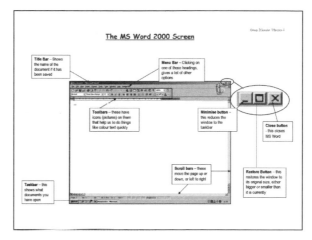

The MS Word screen handout

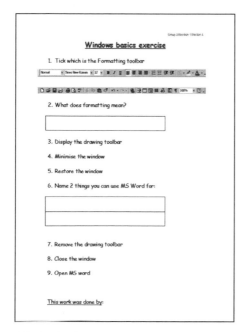

Window basics exercise

Section 5

Resources: Computer components picture cards; Blank MS Word screen disk work

Pictures can be held up for learners to say what they are.
The blank MS Word screen can be filled in either on disk or on paper.

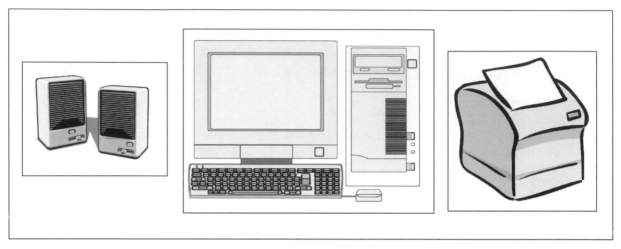

Computer components picture cards

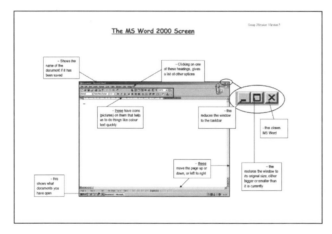

Blank MS Word screen disk work

Section 6

Resources: Word processing checklist; How to highlight text handout; Undo button, Font Style and Font Size large icon cards; Change the size and style exercise

The checklist is for learners to fill in when they feel confident in a new skill they have learnt. The checklist has two benefits: firstly for learners to see their own achievements and secondly for tutors to see what areas to concentrate on for that person.

You may need to explain how to use the Shift key for capital letters.

There are many different ways to highlight text. It is better to show one way as opposed to all the different ways to highlight. This may depend on the learner's physical ability to use the mouse.

When demonstrating how to change the font style and size, use their name that they typed earlier in this section.

To use the size and name cards, give learners next to each other different cards so that when they have finished using their cards they can swap with the person next to them.

Word processing checklist

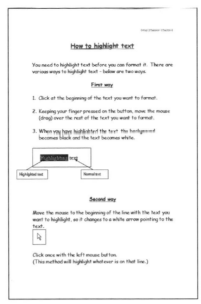

How to highlight text handout

Font style large icon card

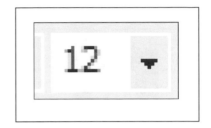

Font Size large icon card

Change the size and style exercise

Undo large icon card

Section 7

Resources: Bold, Italic and Underline large icon card: BIU disk work

You can use the learner's name, which was typed earlier. You will need to make sure the font style is not one that is already emphasised, such as Arial Black or Impact.

Bold, Italic and Underline large icon card

BIU disk work

Tutor notes: Group 2/Session 2

Section 1

Resources: Components recap disk work; Bold, Italic and Underline, Undo, Font Size and Font Style large icon cards; Word basics disk work; Icons handout

With the icons handout, the learners should only fill in the icons they know, and have used, not all of them at once. This will help to reinforce the known icons.

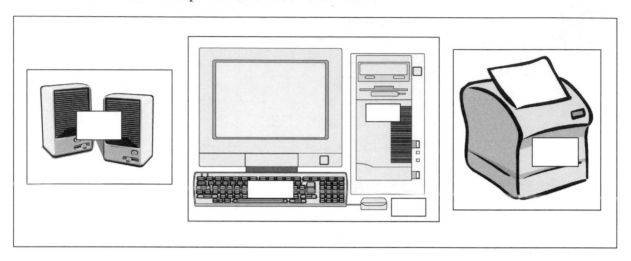

Components recap disk work

Bold, Italic and Underline large icon card

Undo large icon card

Font Size large icon card

Font style large icon card

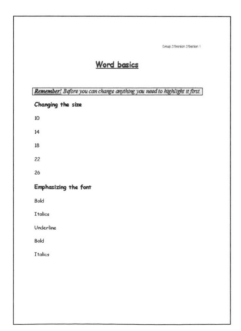

Window basics disk work

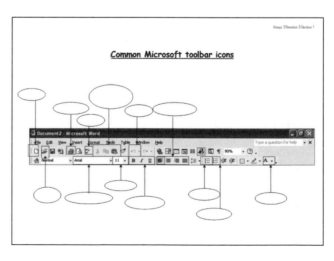

Icons handout

Section 2

Resources: Inserting 1 disk work and worksheet

Make sure learners know where to put the insertion point when inserting text. Try to let learners guess where to put the insertion point for the second sentence.

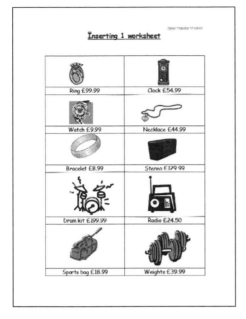

Inserting 1 worksheet

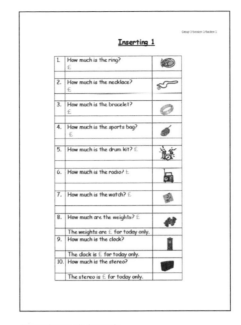

Inserting 1 disk work

Section 3

Resources: Inserting 1 disk work and worksheet

It is better to use one method of deleting to avoid confusion, depending on your learner group. Either use the Backspace key, Delete key or highlighting the text and pressing delete. If some learners already have a preferred way of deleting, you do not need to change that.

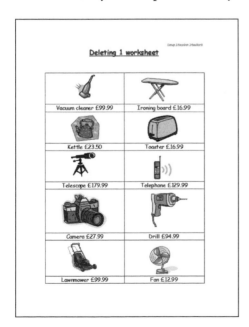

Deleting 1 worksheet

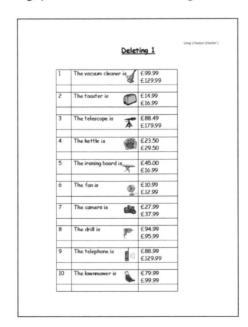

Deleting 1 disk work

Section 4

Resources: New Page large icon card; Saving a document handout

At this stage, using File and then Save As can avoid the loss of some work as it gets learners to add a filename as opposed to saving work on top of what is already there, as would happen with the Save icon or command.

The saving exercise is supposed to introduce saving to your learners. They will be saving lots of work during the course, where the saving procedure can be reinforced.

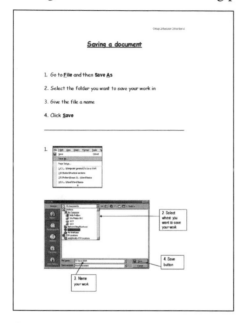

Saving a document handout

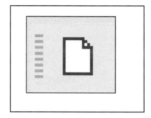

New Page large icon card

Section 5

Resources: Opening a document handout

When recapping the procedure on how to save and open a document, the points can be written on the whiteboard/flipchart for extra reference.

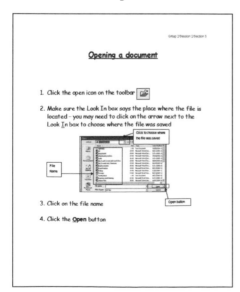

Opening a document handout

Section 6

Resources: About me disk work; About my lesson disk work; Session 2 worksheet

This section gives you the chance to assess the skills learnt and to help learners individually.

About me disk work

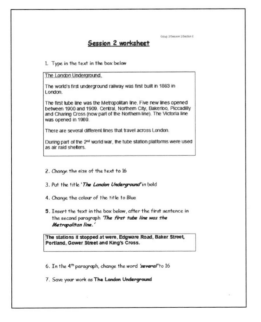

Session 2 worksheet

76   ICT FOR LEARNERS WITH SPECIAL NEEDS

Tutor notes: Group 2/Session 3

Section 1

Resources: Inserting 2 disk work; Deleting 2 disk work; New Page and Open large icon cards

When eliciting information from learners, try to write the details on a board or flipchart.
For Inserting 2, learners should insert the item (from the pictures provided in the exercise) into the sentence.

For Deleting 2, learners need to delete the incorrect item.

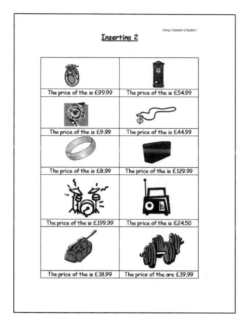

Inserting 2 disk work

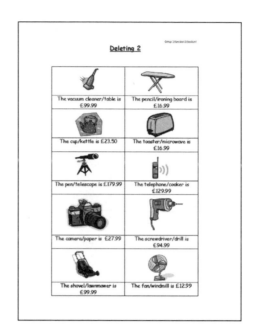

Deleting 2 disk work

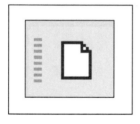

New Page large icon card

Open large icon card

Section 2

Resources: Alignment large icon card; Alignments example sheet; Alignment practice disk work

The alignments example sheet is to give learners a visual aid to see the differences in how the buttons affect the text.

When using the learner's name to show how the alignment buttons work, you will not be able to use the justified button.

Alignments example sheet

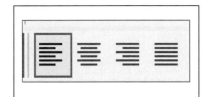

Alignment large icon card

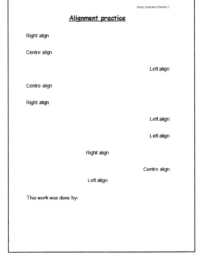

Alignment practice disk work

Section 3

Resources: Font Colour large icon card; Colour and alignment practice disk work

Font Colour large icon card

Colour and alignment practice disk work

Section 4

Resources: Matching the icons 1 worksheet

This section gives you the chance to assess the skills learnt and to help learners with any individual needs.

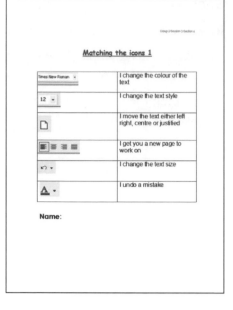

Matching the icons 1 worksheet

Adverts example sheet

Section 5

Resources: Adverts example sheet; Flyer/Invitation examples

Learners can either copy from one of the examples or create an advert/flyer etc. of their own. This will also consolidate how they can use the skills for their own work.

Flyer example

Invitation example

Tutor notes: Group 3/Session 1

Sections 1–3

Resources: Computer components handout; How to turn on the computer handout

See Tutor notes for Group 2/Session 1/Sections 1–3.

Section 4

Resources: Mouse control skills 1 and 2 disk work

See Tutor notes for Group 1/Session 1/Section 4.

Section 5

Resources: SEMERC Assessability software

This software helps to determine your learners' strengths and weaknesses. Some learners may feel confident to complete the assessment without any input; others may need clarification on what is being asked of them.

It would be beneficial to have a look at the disk so you know what your learners will have to do. If the computers at the centre do not have sound you will have to explain the requirements of the disk, as it uses audio for the instructions.

A discussion with the class after the first section of the assessment helps to break up the concentration needed to complete the assessment and also give you a chance to find out how your learners are coping with the assessment.

Adaptation: You can hold up cards for the learners with multiple choice questions which they fill in either on the computer or on a printed sheet.

SEMERC Assessability software

Tutor notes: Group 3/Session 2

Section 1

Resources: **Components recap disk work**

See Tutor notes for Group 2/Session 2/Section 1.

Section 2

Resources: **SEMERC Assessability software**

Section 3

Resources: **Computer components jigsaw; How to turn on the computer cut out sheet; Scissors**

You will need to print the computer components picture on to card which can be laminated and then cut out.

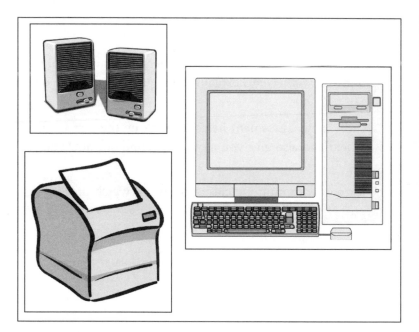

Computer components jigsaw

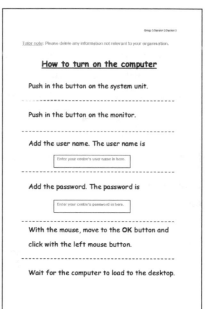

How to turn on the computer cut out sheet

For the 'How to turn on the computer' instructions, cut the individual instructions into strips for learners to put back into order.

Section 4

Resources: **SEMERC Assessability software**

Section 5

Resources: **Typing skills program**

There are various typing programs available to help with letter recognition such as the Touch Type software from Iota.

It is not necessary to concentrate on which fingers they are using for each key. The focus for this exercise is on finding the correct letters.

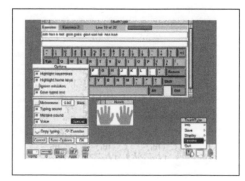

Tutor notes: Group 3/Session 3

Section 1

Resources: Internet connection; How to log on to the internet handout; Internet Explorer web browser handout; Web addresses worksheet

When logging on to the internet, it may be easier to use the Internet Explorer icon on the Taskbar if you have one as it only requires one click. This icon has been used in the resources, so if you use a different way to establish an internet connection you will need to change this.

When looking at the browser features, highlight the common features such as the browser window and address bar.

For the web address worksheet you can use web addresses that are country based, especially if English is not the first language for your learners.

How to log on to the internet handout

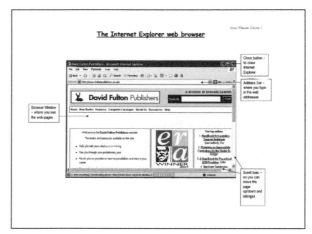

Internet Explorer web browser handout

Web addresses worksheet

Section 2

Resources: Internet connection; Using links exercise

Before using the exercise, check that all links are working properly as websites change their information from time to time.

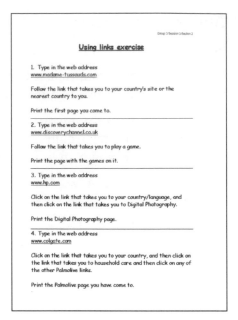

Using links exercise

Section 3

Resources: Internet basics quiz

This can be done as a group or individual exercise, verbally or written, with the answers given at the end.

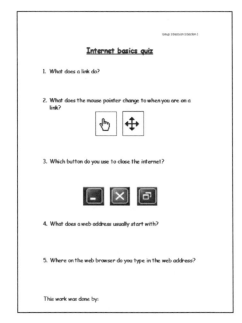

Internet basics quiz

Section 4

Resources: Internet connection

This section is to help learners build on skills learnt earlier and encourages them to think and act independently about topics that interest them.

Section 5

Resources: Typing skills program

Section 3

Useful information

Equipment and providers

Overview

There is a wide range of equipment available to help aid ICT learning. Some of the these are described below.

Mouse alternatives

- Optical mouse – this is a mouse that does not use a ball. This means there is no sticking or cleaning of the mouse ball required.
- SEMERC Roller 2 and Roller 2 Plus – the rollers have coloured buttons with a removable keyguard that prevents unwanted pressing of buttons.
- Joysticks – help with the movement of the mouse pointer, double-clicking and dragging screen items.

Switches

These work in conjunction with special software. Switches are stationary and the whole surface can be pressed for a response.

Monitors

You can purchase monitors with built-in touch screens, or touch screens that attach to existing monitors so learners can select items on the screen directly with fingers instead of a mouse.

Keyboards

The variety of keyboards available includes:

- big key keyboards and coloured key keyboards to help the visually impaired
- keyboards with trackballs attached
- key skins, which protect the keyboard against spills, and are available in upper or lower case
- keyguards, can prevent accidental pressing of keys close to the key required
- high-visibility stickers are high contrast stickers that can be attached to any keyboard or peripheral device for identification.

Below is a list of some providers of ICT equipment and software for individuals with special needs.

Hardware

Blazie

Windermere House, Kendal Avenue, London W3 0XA, UK
Tel: +44 (0) 20 8752 8650, Fax: +44 (0) 20 8752 8658
Email: barry.webb@blazie.co.uk
Web: www.blazie.co.uk

The Call Centre

University of Edinburgh, Paterson's Land, Holyrood Road, Edinburgh EH8 8AQ, UK
Tel: +44 (0) 131 651 6235/6236, Fax: +44 (0) 131 651 6234
Email: call.centre@ed.ac.uk
Web: callcentre.education.ed.ac.uk

Computers for the disabled

41 New Waverley Road, Noak Bridge, Laindon, Essex SS15 4BJ, UK
Tel: +44 (0) 1268 284834, Fax: +44 (0) 1268 479028
Email: bigpaulh@blueyonder.co.uk
Web: www.cftd.co.uk

Dynamic Ability

The Coach House, 134 Purewell, Christchurch, Dorset BH23 1EU, UK
Tel: +44 (0) 1202 481818/479955

Easiaids Ltd

5 Woodcote Park Avenue, Purley, Surrey CR8 3NH, UK
Tel and Fax: +44 (0) 20 8763 0203
Email: enquiries@easiaids.co.uk
Web: www.easyaids.co.uk

iANSYST Ltd

Fen House, Fen Road, Cambridge CB4 1UN, UK
Tel: +44 (0) 1223 420101, Fax: +44 (0) 1223 426644
Email: reception@dyslexic.com
Web: www.iansyst.co.uk

Inclusive Technology Ltd

Gatehead Business Park, Delph New Road, Delph, Oldham OL3 5BX, UK
Tel: +44 (0) 1457 819790, Fax: +44 (0) 1457 819799
Email: inclusive@inclusive.co.uk
Web: www.inclusive.co.uk

US site

Inclusive TLC, 315 Wootton Street, Unit A, Boonton, NJ 07005, USA
Tel: 1 800 462 0930 (USA), +1 973 331 9898, Fax: +1 973 331 9849
Email: info@inclusiveTLC.com
Web: www.inclusivetlc.com

Keytools Ltd

Tools for the Computer Enabled, Freepost, Southampton SO17 1YA, UK
Tel: +44 (0) 23 8058 4314, Fax: +44 (0) 23 8055 6902
Email: info@keytools.com
Web: www.keytools.com

Learning Works International

9 Barrow Close, Marlborough, Wiltshire SN8 2BD, UK
Tel: +44 (0) 1672 512914, Fax: +44 (0) 1672 519025
Email: info@learning-works.org.uk
Web: www.learning-works.org.uk

Liberator Ltd

Whitegates, Swinstead NG33 4PA, UK
Tel: +44 (0) 1476 550391
Email: sales@liberator.co.uk
Web: www.liberator.co.uk

Maxess Products Ltd

The Chinestone, Dancers Hill, Charlbury, Oxfordshire OX7 3RZ, UK
Tel and fax: +44 (0) 1608 811909
Email: sales@maxessproducts.co.uk
Web: www.maxessproducts.co.uk

Modern World Data Ltd

Arran House, Arran Road, Dolgellau, Gwynedd LL40 1HW, UK
Tel: +44 (0) 1341 422044 or +44 (0) 1341 422083
Email: info@modern-world-data.com
Web: www.modern-world-data.com

PCD Maltron Ltd

15 Orchard Lane, East Molesey, Surrey KT8 0BN, UK
Tel and Fax: +44 (0) 20 8398 3265
Email: sales@maltron.com
Web: www.maltron.com

Quality Enabling Devices – QED

1 Prince Albert Street, Gosport, Hampshire PO12 1QH, UK
Tel: 0870 787 8850, Fax: 0870 787 8860
Email: sales@qedltd.com
Web: www.qedltd.com

Research Machines

RM plc, Unit 140 Milton Park, Abingdon, Oxon OX14 4SE, UK
Tel: 0870 920 0200, Fax: +44 (0) 1235 826999
Web: www.rm.com

SEMERC

London

Granada Learning, The Chiswick Centre, 414 Chiswick High Road, London W4 5TF, UK
Tel: +44 (0) 20 8996 3333, Fax: +44 (0) 20 8742 8390

Manchester

Granada Learning, Granada Television, Quay Street, Manchester M60 9EA, UK
Tel: +44 (0) 161 827 2927, Fax: +44 (0) 161 827 2966

Newcastle

Granada Learning, Tyne Tees Studios, City Road, Newcastle Upon Tyne NE1 2AL, UK

SEMERC Information Services

Tel: +44 (0) 161 827 2719
Email: info@semerc.com
Web: www.semerc.com

SEN Marketing – Bookshop

618 Leeds Road, Outwood, Wakefield WF1 2LT, UK
Tel and Fax: +44 (0) 1924 871697
Email: info@sen.uk.com
Web: www.sen.uk.com

Sight and Sound Technology

Qantel House, Anglia Way, Moulton Park, Northampton NN3 6JA, UK
Tel: 0845 634 7979 (UK local rate), +44 (0) 1604 798070, Fax: +44 (0) 1604 798090
Email: sales@sightandsound.co.uk
Web: www.sightandsound.co.uk

Software

Attainment

Software for children and adults with special needs, from maths to work skills, distributed worldwide
Tel: 1 800 327 4269 (USA), +1 608 845 7880
Email: info@attainmentcompany.com, Dan@attainmentcompany.com (international sales)
Web: www.attainmentcompany.com

Cambridgeshire Software House

Educational software for all age ranges
PO Box 163, Huntingdon, Cambridgeshire PE28 3UR, UK
Tel: +44 (0) 1487 741223, Fax: +44 (0) 1487 741213
Email: sales@cshsoft.com
Web: www.cshsoft.com

Crick Software

Easy-to-use reading and writing software for children and adults with special needs

UK

Crick Software Ltd, Crick House, Boarden Close, Moulton Park, Northampton NN3 6LF, UK
Tel: +44 (0) 1604 671691, Fax: +44 (0) 1604 671692
Email: info@cricksoft.com
Web: www.cricksoft.com/uk

US Address

50 116th Ave SE, Suite 211, Bellevue, WA 98004, USA
Tel: 1 866 33 CRICK (US toll-free), +1 425 467 8260, Fax: +1 425 467 8245
Email: info@cricksoft.com
Web: www.cricksoft.com

Dolphin Systems

Software for the visually impaired

Europe and Asia

Dolphin Computer Access Ltd, Technology House, Blackpole Estate West, Worcester WR3 8TJ, UK
Tel: +44 (0) 1905 754 577, 0845 130 5353 (UK local rate), Fax: +44 (0) 1905 754 559
Email: info@dolphinuk.co.uk
Web: www.dolphinuk.co.uk

USA and Canada

Dolphin Computer Access, 60 East Third Avenue, Suite 301, San Mateo, CA 94401, USA
Tel: +1 650 348 7401, +1 866 797 5921 (toll-free), Fax: +1 650 348 7403
Email: info@dolphinusa.com
Web: www.dolphinusa.com

Scandinavia and the Baltic states

Labyrinten Data AB, Box 132, 52102 Falköping, Sweden
Tel: +46 (0) 5158 2175, Fax: +46 (0) 5158 0847
Email: office@dolphinse.com
Web: www.dolphinse.com

Education by Design

Inspirational ideas and information for teachers, therapists and parents, to encourage children and
adults with special needs with intellectual disabilities to reach their full potential
Email: info@edbydesign.com
Web: www.edbydesign.com

Iota Software

Animator software
Iota Software Ltd, PO Box 837, Cambridge CB5 0ZN, UK
Tel: +44 (0) 1223 566 789, +44 (0) 1223 566789, Fax: +44 (0) 1223 566788
Email: info@iota.co.uk
Web: www.iota.co.uk

Laureate Learning Systems

Special needs software
Laureate Learning Systems, Inc., 110 East Spring Street, Winooski, VT 05404-1898, USA
Tel: 1 800 562 6801 (USA), +1 802 655 4755, Fax:+1 802 655 4757
Email: customer-service@laureatelearning.com
Web: www.llsys.com

One Stop Education

Software products and resources from SEMERC and Granada Learning
Tel: 0845 6021937 (UK local rate)
Email: info@onestopeducation.co.uk
Web: www.onestopeducation.co.uk

Penfriend Ltd

Penfriend XP helps dyslexic and physically disabled people to write faster by predicting the next word they want
30 South Oswald Road, Edinburgh EH9 2HG, UK
Tel: +44 (0) 131 668 2000, Fax: +44 (0) 131 668 2121
Email: sales@penfriend.biz
Web: www.penfriend.ltd.uk

Propeller Multimedia Ltd

Software designed for stroke rehabilitation and brain injury patients. The software helps with speech, reading, writing and cognitive skills
PO Box 13791, Peebles EH45 9YR, UK
Tel and Fax: +44 (0) 1896 833528
Email: enquiries@propeller.net
Web: www.propeller.net/rehab

R-E-M

Educational software online store
Great Western House, Langport, Somerset TA10 9YU, UK
Tel: +44 (0) 1458 254700, Fax: +44 (0) 1458 254701
Email: Info@R-E-M.co.uk
Web: www.r-e-m.co.uk

Resource

Software for special needs learners
51 High Street, Kegworth, Derby DE74 2DA, UK
Tel: 0870 777 0247, +44 (0) 1509 672222, Fax: +44 (0) 1509 672267
Email: ws2@resourcekt.co.uk
Web: www.resourcekt.co.uk

Texthelp Systems

Software products designed to assist individuals to improve their reading and writing abilities
Tel: 0800 328 7910 (UK toll-free), +44 (0) 28 9442 8105, Fax: +44 (0) 28 9442 8574
US toll-free voicemail: +1 888 333 9907, US toll-free fax: +1 877 631 5991
Email: info@texthelp.com
Web: www.texthelp.com

Widgit Software

Symbols software
124 Cambridge Science Park, Milton Road, Cambridge CB4 0ZS, UK
Tel: +44 (0) 1223 425558, Fax +44 (0) 1223 425349
Email: sales@widgit.com
Web: www.widgit.com

Wordshark

Literacy and numeracy software especially suitable for people with dyslexia
White Space, 41 Mall Rd, London W6 9DG, UK
Tel: + 44 (0) 20 8748 5927, Fax: + 44 (0) 20 8748 5927
Email: tigg@wordshark.co.uk
Web: www.wordshark.co.uk

Xavier Educational Software

Computer-based teaching aids for English language, early learning and dyslexia
School of Psychology, University of Wales, Bangor, Gwynedd LL57 2AS, UK
Tel: +44 (0) 1248 382616, Fax: +44 (0) 1248 382599
Email: xavier@bangor.ac.uk
Web: www.xavier.bangor.ac.uk

Qualifications

This section highlights some of the qualifications available for learners who wish to receive a certificate in their use of computers.

It may be more beneficial and cost effective to consult your local further education (FE) college or local education organisation about the courses they have available rather than your own organisation becoming a test centre for learners to take exams. This can be expensive, especially if you only have a few students who are interested in taking their learning further.

It is advisable for learners to take a numeracy/literacy diagnostic assessment (an assessment that gauges the needs of students in terms of numeracy or literacy skills), which could be done in conjunction with the course provider to ensure learners are getting any extra help needed to complete the exams. You can also enquire about extra time for learners with special needs to complete the exams.

The City and Guilds of London Institute

City and Guilds is a leading vocational awarding body in the UK, awarding almost 50% of all national vocational qualifications (NVQs). They are also a global organisation, providing unique internationally recognised qualifications across the world through City and Guilds International.

City and Guilds offers a range of ICT courses from beginners to intermediate.

Your local FE college will have details on the City and Guilds courses they offer.

European Computer Driving Licence

The European Computer Driving Licence® (ECDL) is the internationally recognised qualification which enables people to demonstrate their competence in computer skills. It is the fastest-growing IT user qualification in over 125 countries.

The ECDL consists of seven modules:

- Basic concepts of IT
- Using the computer and managing files
- Word processing
- Spreadsheets
- Database
- Presentation
- Information and communication.

After completing each module exam, proof is written in a logbook. Learners have a time-scale of three years to complete all seven modules to receive the full certificate.

For information on becoming a test centre or to find one local to you visit the ECDL website at www.ecdl.com.

Microsoft Office User Specialist (MOUS)

Microsoft Office Specialist certification, the premier Microsoft desktop certification, is a globally recognised standard for demonstrating desktop skills. To earn the Microsoft Office Specialist certification for Microsoft Office or Microsoft Project, you must pass one or more certification exams. Office Specialist exams provide a valid and reliable measure of technical proficiency and expertise by evaluating your overall comprehension of Office or Microsoft Project programs, your ability to use their advanced features, and your ability to integrate the Office programs with other software programs. Details of centres worldwide that offer this exam can be found at www.microsoft.com/learning/mcp/officespecialist/default.asp.

National Open College Network (NOCN) – UK

The National Open College Network (NOCN) is a provider of accreditation services for adult learning. NOCN is a recognised national qualification awarding body and is the central organisation for 28 Open College Networks (OCNs) based across the UK.

NOCN provides national qualifications and programmes in a wide range of subject areas and offers a local accreditation service through the OCNs that provides recognition of achievement through the awarding of credit.

All OCNs work within a common framework of accreditation consisting of:

- a set of levels consistent with the national framework
- a unit structure
- a credit value for each unit.

This enables clear identification of what is being learned, recognition of the achievement of learners as and when it happens, and flexibility, both in terms of what is delivered and how it is achieved.

Accreditation is offered through your local Open College Network (OCN) with local staff to support you through the process. You will need to contact your local OCN if you are thinking of submitting a programme for accreditation. Details of your local OCN can be found at www.nocn.org.uk.

Oxford, Cambridge and RSA (OCR) examinations – Computer Literacy And Information Technology (CLAIT) – UK

The OCR Computer Literacy and Information Technology (CLAIT) exam has three levels: new CLAIT beginners, CLAIT plus and CLAIT advanced. There are various units including:

- Using a computer
- Word processing
- Electronic communication
- Spreadsheets
- Database
- Desktop publishing
- Graphs and charts
- Web pages
- Graphical presentations
- BBC Becoming WebWise.

More details can be found at www.ocr.org.uk.

Useful organisations

Below is a list of organisations that specialise in help and advice on mental health and disability needs. Some are based in the UK with links to other countries but all have valuable information and ideas for all nationalities.

AbilityNet

Charity bringing the benefits of computer technology to adults and children with disabilities. Provides a wide range of services to individuals and professionals in the field of disability, employment and the public sector

PO Box 94, Warwick CV34 5WS, UK
Tel: 0800 269545 (UK toll-free), Fax +44 (0) 1926 407425
Email: enquiries@abilitynet.org.uk
Web: www.abilitynet.org.uk

Action for ME

Dedicated to improving the lives of people with ME

PO Box 1302, Wells, Somerset BA5 1YE, UK
Tel: +44 (0) 1749 670799, Fax: +44 (0) 1749 672561
Email: admin@afme.org.uk
Web: www.afme.org.uk

Arthritis Care

Voluntary organisation working with and for people with arthritis. They aim to empower people to take control of their arthritis and their lives

18 Stephenson Way, London NW1 2HD, UK
Tel: +44 (0) 20 7380 6500, Fax: +44 (0) 20 7380 6505
Web: www.arthritiscare.org.uk

Basic Skills for Inclusive Learning

Internet site to support tutors and others who are helping adults who have learning difficulties and/or disabilities to learn

Web: www.ctad.co.uk/basil

British Association of Services to the Elderly (BASE)

Provides training in the care of older people and other adults who need care and support. They offer a wide range of professional training and career development, as well as consultancy and facilitation services

The Guildford Institute, Ward Street, Guildford GU1 4LH, UK
Tel: +44 (0) 1483 451036, Fax: +44 (0) 1483 451034
Email: enquiries@basc.org.uk
Web: www.base.org.uk

British Association of Teachers of the Deaf

The professional association for teachers of the deaf

175 Dashwood Avenue, High Wycombe, Buckinghamshire HP12 3DB, UK
Tel and Fax: +44 (0) 1494 464190
Email: secretary@batod.org.uk
Web: www.batod.org.uk

British Computer Society Disability Group

The BCS Disability Group focuses on the role of IT in giving disabled people a better quality of life

Tel: +44 (0) 1245 363993
Email: disability.grp@bcs.org.uk
Web: www.bcs.org/BCS/Groups/SpecialistGroups/DtoE/DisabilityGroup/default.htm

British Dyslexia Association

The BDA's role has been raising awareness of the evidence and effects of dyslexia. They now also aim to develop and encourage services that meet the needs of dyslexic people

98 London Road, Reading RG1 5AU, UK
Tel: +44 (0) 118 966 2677, Fax: +44 (0) 118 935 1927
Email: info@dyslexiahelp-bda.demon.co.uk
Web: www.bda-dyslexia.org.uk

British Educational Communications and Technology Agency (Becta)

A UK agency that supports all four UK education departments in their strategic ICT developments

Millburn Hill Road, Science Park, Coventry CV4 7JJ, UK
Tel: +44 (0) 24 7641 6994, Fax: +44 (0) 24 7641 1418
Email: becta@becta.org.uk
Web: www.becta.org.uk

British Educational Suppliers Association (BESA)

BESA produces an annual directory of members known as the BESAbook to guide you to the right educational suppliers for your needs

20 Beaufort Court, Admirals Way, London E14 9XL, UK
Tel: +44 (0) 20 7537 4997, Fax: +44 (0) 20 7537 4846
Email: besa@besa.org.uk
Web: www.besanet.org.uk

British Institute of Learning Disabilities

Organisation committed to improving the quality of life for the 1.2 million people in the UK with a learning disability

Campion House, Green Street, Kidderminster, Worcestershire DY10 1JL, UK
Tel: +44 (0) 1562 723010, Fax: +44 (0) 1562 723029
Email: enquiries@bild.org.uk
Web: www.bild.org.uk

The Centre for Independent Living

A collection of key services for disabled people

Arthur Richardson Resource Centre, Savoy Road, Hull HU8 0TX, UK
Tel: +44 (0) 1482 788668, Fax: +44 (0) 1482 719590, Textphone: +44 (0) 1482 719591
Web: www.choicesandrights.org.uk

Communication Matters UK

National charitable organisation of members concerned with the augmentative and alternative communication (AAC) needs of people with complex communication needs

c/o The ACE Centre, 92 Windmill Road, Oxford OX3 7DR, UK
Tel and Fax: 0845 456 8211 (UK local rate), +44 (0)131 554 0218
Email: admin@communicationmatters.org.uk
Web: www.communicationmatters.org.uk

Directions Plus

Information service for disabled people and their carers who live or work in Cambridge, East Cambridgeshire, South Cambridgeshire and Fenland

Orwell House, Cowley Road, Cambridge CB4 0PP, UK
Tel: 0800 269 545 (UK toll-free), Fax: +44 (0) 1223 506 470, Textphone: +44 (0) 1926 312847
Email: info@directions-plus.org.uk
Web: www.directions-plus.org.uk

Disability Information Service (DISS)

A national Database of disability information

Harrowlands Centre, Harrowlands Park, Dorking, Surrey RH4 2RA, UK
Tel: +44 (0) 1306 742282, Fax: +44 (0) 1306 741740
Email: diss@diss.org.uk
Web: www.diss.org.uk

Disabled Living Foundation (DLF)

The DLF has been working for freedom, empowerment and choice for disabled and older people and others who use equipment or assistive technologies (AT) to enhance their independence

380–384 Harrow Road, London W9 2HU, UK
Tel: +44 (0) 20 7289 6111, Textphone: +44 (0) 20 7432 8009
Web: www.dlf.org.uk

Down's Syndrome Association

An organisation focusing on all aspects of living successfully with Down's syndrome

Langdon Down Centre, 2a Langdon Park, Teddington TW11 9PS, UK
Tel: 0845 230 0372 (UK local rate), Fax: 0845 230 0373 (UK local rate)
Email: info@downs-syndrome.org.uk
Web: www.downs-syndrome.org.uk

Dyslexia Institute

An educational charity for the assessment and teaching of people with dyslexia and for the training of teachers

Head Office and National Training and Resource Centre, Park House, Wick Road, Egham, Surrey TW20 0HH, UK
Tel: +44 (0) 1784 222300, Fax: +44 (0) 1784 222333
Email: info@dyslexia-inst.org.uk
Web: www.dyslexia-inst.org.uk

Dyslexia Research Trust

Set up to fund cutting-edge interdisciplinary research into dyslexia and other related conditions and to support free clinics to assess and assist people with these conditions

Dyslexia Research Trust, 65 Kingston Road, Oxford OX2 6RJ, UK
Tel: +44 (0) 1865 552303
Email: info@dyslexic.org.uk
Web: www.dyslexic.org.uk

Dyspraxia Foundation

A UK charity which exists to help people to understand and cope with dyspraxia. It is a resource for parents, teenagers and adults who have the condition, and also for professionals

8 West Alley, Hitchin, Herts SG5 1EG, UK
Tel: +44 (0) 1462 454986, Fax: +44 (0) 1462 455052
Email: dyspraxia@dyspraxiafoundation.org.uk
Web: www.dyspraxiafoundation.org.uk

ICT Consortium

A group of voluntary sector organisations who have come together to plan and deliver a coordinated framework of ICT guidance, good practice, advice and support for voluntary and community organisations, accessible at a local level

Tel: +44 (0) 20 7520 2509
Email: catherine.archer@ncvo-vol.org.uk
Web: www.ictconsortium.org.uk

Learning and Teaching Scotland

An executive non-departmental public body sponsored by the Scottish Executive Education Department to help review, assess and support developments in learning and education, including the use of information and communication technology

74 Victoria Crescent Road, Glasgow G12 9JN, UK
Tel: +44 (0) 141 337 5000
Gardyne Road, Dundee DD5 1NY, UK
Tel: +44 (0) 1382 443600
Email: enquiries@LTScotland.org.uk
Web: www.ltscotland.org.uk

Makaton Vocabulary Development Project

Makaton is a unique language programme offering a structured, multi-modal approach for the teaching of communication, language and literacy skills. Devised for children and adults with a variety of communication and learning disabilities, Makaton is used extensively throughout the UK and has been adapted for use in over 40 other countries

31 Firwood Drive, Camberley, Surrey GU15 3QD, UK
Tel: +44 (0) 1276 61390, Fax: +44 (0) 1276 681368
Email: mvdp@makaton.org
Web: www.makaton.org

Manic Depression Fellowship

A national user-led registered charity for people whose lives are affected by manic depression

Castle Works, 21 St George's Road, London SE1 6ES, UK
Tel: 0845 634 0540 (UK local rate), Fax: +44 (0) 20 7793 2639
Email mdf@mdf.org.uk
Web: www.mdf.org.uk

Mental Health Foundation

Offers the latest news and events on mental health issues, as well as information on problems, treatments and strategies for living with mental distress

7th Floor, 83 Victoria Street, London SW1H 0HW
Tel: + 44 (0) 20 7802 0300. Fax: + 44 (0) 20 7802 0301
Email: mhf@mhf.org.uk
5th Floor, Merchants House, 30 George Square, Glasgow G2 1EG
Tel: + 44 (0) 141 572 0125. Fax + 44 (0) 141 572 0246
Email: scotland@mhf.org.uk
www.mentalhealth.org.uk

Mind

Mental health charity in England and Wales that work to create a better life for everyone with experience of mental distress by advancing the views, needs and ambitions of people with mental health problems, challenging discrimination and promoting inclusion, influencing policy through campaigning and education, inspiring the development of quality services which reflect expressed need and diversity, and achieving equal rights through campaigning and education.

PO Box 277, Manchester M60 3XN, UK
Tel: 0845 766 0163 (UK local rate)
Email: info@mind.org.uk
Web: www.mind.org.uk

National Association for Special Educational Needs (NASEN)

A leading organisation in the UK which aims to promote the education, training, advancement and development of all those with special educational needs

NASEN House, 4/5 Amber Business Village, Amber Close, Amington, Tamworth, Staffordshire B77 4RP, UK
Tel: +44 (0) 1827 311500, Fax: +44 (0) 1827 313005
Email: welcome@nasen.org.uk
Web: www.nasen.org.uk

National Grid for Learning (NGfL)

The NGfL provides a network of selected links to websites that offer high-quality content and information, whether you are learning, supporting, teaching or managing

Web: www.ngfl.gov.uk

National Institute of Adult Continuing Education (NIACE)

A non-governmental organisation working for adult learners

NIACE, Renaissance House, 20 Princess Road West, Leicester LE1 6TP, UK
Tel: +44 (0)116 204 4200/4201, Fax: +44 (0) 116 285 4514
Email: enquiries@niace.org.uk
NIACE Dysgu Cymru, 3rd Floor, 35 Cathedral Road, Cardiff CF11 9HB, Wales, UK
Tel: +44 (0) 29 2037 0900, Fax: +44 (0) 29 2037 0909
Email: enquiries@niacedc.org.uk
Web: www.niace.org.uk/default.htm

Paradigm

A consultancy and development agency with a difference – formed by people with experience in inclusion, health, social services, community care and organisational development

Paradigm, 8 Brandon Street, Birkenhead CH41 5HN, UK
Tel: 0870 010 4933, Fax: 0870 010 4934
Email: admin@paradigm-uk.org
Web: www.paradigm-uk.org

Pavilion publishing

A specialist source of training resources, magazines and journals, courses, events, conferences and exhibitions for professionals in health and social care. Their aim is to improve the lives of those who use health, social care and other related services by maximising the training opportunities of professionals who work with them

The Ironworks, Cheapside, Brighton, East Sussex BN1 4GD, UK
Tel: 0870 161 3505, +44 (0) 1273 623222, Fax: + 44 (0) 1273 625526
Email: info@pavpub.com
Web: www.pavpub.com

The Psychiatry Research Trust

Formed with the sole aim of raising funds for research into mental illness and brain disease

Box 8, De Crespigny Park, Denmark Hill, London SE5 8AF, UK
Tel: +44 (0) 20 7703 6217, Fax: +44 (0) 20 7848 5115
Email: s.refault@iop.kcl.ac.uk
Web: www.iop.kcl.ac.uk/iop/prt/default.htm

Pyramid Educational Consultants UK Ltd

Provides training, consultation and support to parents, carers and professionals involved with children and adults with communication difficulties

Pavilion House, 6 Old Steine, Brighton BN1 1EJ, UK
Tel: +44 (0) 1273 609555, Fax: +44 (0) 1273 609556
Email: pyramid@pecs.org.uk
Web: www.pecs.org.uk

Rethink Disability Ltd

Charity that represents disabled people on a wide range of voluntary and statutory committees involving the planning and provision of services for disabled people at local, divisional and county level

Red Gables, Ipswich Road, Stowmarket, Suffolk IP14 1BE, UK
Tel: +44 (0) 1449 770127, Fax: +44 (0) 1449 770135, Minicom: +44 (0) 1449 775999
Email: enquiries@rethink-disability.org.uk
Web: www.rethink-disability.org.uk

Royal National Institute of the Blind (RNIB)

RNIB help anyone with a sight problem – not just with braille, talking books and computer training, but with imaginative and practical solutions to everyday challenges

105 Judd Street, London WC1H 9NE, UK
Tel: +44 (0) 20 7388 1266, Fax: +44 (0) 20 7388 2034
Email: helpline@rnib.org.uk
Web: www.rnib.org.uk

Royal National Institute for the Deaf (RNID)

The largest charity representing the 9 million deaf and hard-of-hearing people in the UK. As a membership charity, they aim to achieve a better quality of life for deaf and hard-of-hearing people, including campaigning and lobbying to change laws and government policies, providing information and raising awareness of deafness, hearing loss and tinnitus, and training courses and consultancy on deafness and disability

19–23 Featherstone Street, London EC1Y 8SL, UK
Tel: 0808 808 0123 (toll-free), Fax: +44 (0) 20 7296 8199, Textphone: 0808 808 9000 (toll-free)
Email: informationline@rnid.org
Web: www.rnid.org.uk

The Salnsbury Centre for Mental Health

A charity that works to improve the quality of life for people with severe mental health problems. It carries out research, development and training work to influence policy and practice in health and social care

134 Borough High Street, London SE1 1LB, UK
Tel: +44 (0) 20 7827 8300
Email: contact@scmh.co.uk
Web: www.scmh.org.uk

Sane

A charity that raises awareness and respect for people with mental illness and their families, improve education and training, and secures better services. Sane undertakes research into the causes of serious mental illness through The Prince of Wales International Centre for SANE Research. It provides information and emotional support to those experiencing mental health problems, their families and carers through SANELINE (0845 767 8000, UK local rate)

1st Floor Cityside House, 40 Adler Street, London E1 1EE, UK
Tel: +44 (0) 20 7375 1002, Fax: +44 (0) 20 7375 2162
Email: london@sane.org.uk
Units 1 and 2, The Greenway Centre, Doncaster Road, Southmead, Bristol BS10 5PY, UK
Tel: +44 (0) 117 950 2140, Fax: +44 (0) 117 950 2150
Email: Bristol@sane.org.uk
1 Queen Victoria Street, Macclesfield SK11 6LP, UK
Tel: +44 (0) 1625 429050, Fax: +44 (0) 1625 424975
Email: macclesfield@sane.org.uk
Web: www.sane.org.uk

Scope

A disability organisation in England and Wales whose focus is people with cerebral palsy. Scope's services focus on four main areas where disabled people face the greatest inequality: early years, education, daily living and work. They also provide local support services which respond to the needs identified by disabled people in their areas

6 Market Road, London N7 9PW, UK
Tel: +44 (0) 20 7619 7100
Email: cphelpline@scope.org.uk
Web: www.scope.org.uk

U Can Do I.T.

A charity which provides computer training for blind, deaf and disabled people in their own homes

U Can Do I.T., Highfield House, 4 Woodfall Street, London SW3 4DJ, UK
Tel/Minicom:+44 (0) 20 7730 7766, Fax: +44 (0) 20 7730 6822
Email: info@ucandoit.org.uk
Web: www.ucandoit.org.uk

United Response (UR)

Supports people with learning difficulties and people with mental health problems across England to live in the community, by supporting people in their own homes and working with people to access training and work opportunities

113–123 Upper Richmond Road, London SW15 2TL, UK
Tel: +44 (0) 20 8246 5200, Fax: +44 (0) 20 8780 9538, Minicom: +44 (0) 20 8785 1706
Email: info@unitedresponse.org.uk
Web: www.unitedresponse.org.uk

Way to Learn

Developed by the Department for Education and Skills (DfES) and partner organisations, it is intended to bring together information that will help adult and potential learners make informed decisions about taking up learning

Tel: 0870 000 2288, Fax: +44 (0) 1928 794248
www.waytolearn.co.uk

Guidelines, policies and acts

This section presents guidelines, policies and acts that affect trainers and learners, nationally and internationally.

Universal Declaration of Human Rights

On 10 December 1948 the General Assembly of the United Nations adopted and proclaimed the Universal Declaration of Human Rights. Following this historic act, the Assembly called upon all Member countries to publicise the text of the Declaration and 'to cause it to be disseminated, displayed, read and expounded principally in schools and other educational institutions, without distinction based on the political status of countries or territories'.

Below are some of the key articles within the Universal Declaration.

Article 1

All human beings are born free and equal in dignity and rights. They are endowed with reason and conscience and should act towards one another in a spirit of brotherhood.

Article 23

(1) Everyone has the right to work, to free choice of employment, to just and favourable conditions of work and to protection against unemployment.

(2) Everyone, without any discrimination, has the right to equal pay for equal work.

(3) Everyone who works has the right to just and favourable remuneration ensuring for himself and his family an existence worthy of human dignity, and supplemented, if necessary, by other means of social protection.

(4) Everyone has the right to form and to join trade unions for the protection of his interests.

Article 26

(1) Everyone has the right to education. Education shall be free, at least in the elementary and fundamental stages. Elementary education shall be compulsory. Technical and professional education shall be made generally available and higher education shall be equally accessible to all on the basis of merit.

(2) Education shall be directed to the full development of the human personality and to the strengthening of respect for human rights and fundamental freedoms. It shall promote understanding, tolerance and friendship among all nations, racial or religious groups, and shall further the activities of the United Nations for the maintenance of peace.

A full list of the articles in the declaration can be found at www.un.org/Overview/rights.html.

Government websites for countries that are members of the United Nations will generally have information about disability and human rights legislation. For example, in the UK the Human Rights Act 1998 enshrines the elements of the Declaration in British law.

European legislation

In Europe, most EU countries have disability legislation following the European Union directive on equal treatment in employment.

The Equal Treatment Directive 2000

The EC Equal Treatment in Employment Directive prohibits direct or indirect discrimination in employment on grounds of disability, age, religion or belief. The directive means that failure to provide a reasonable accommodation (termed reasonable adjustments within the UK Disability Discrimination Act) for a disabled person can constitute discrimination.

This directive required that all EU counties must have civil anti-discrimination legislation protecting disabled people in employment by November 2003, irrespective of employer size. Countries may request extensions to November 2006.

For more details see europa.eu.int/comm/employment_social/index/7003_en.html.

In the European Union, The Resolution of the Council and the Ministers for Education meeting with the Council of 31 May 1990 concerned integration of children and young people with disabilities into ordinary systems of education (Official Journal C 162 of 03.07.1990). See www.europa.eu.int/scadplus/leg/en/cha/c11408.htm.

Increasing use should be made of the educational potential of new technology to aid communication and the development of language skills.

Council resolution of 5 May 2003 on equal opportunities for pupils and students with disabilities in education and training

(Official Journal C 134 of 07.06.2003)

In accordance with the European initiatives of 2001 concerning the European Year of People with Disabilities 2003 (www.europa.eu.int/scadplus/leg/en/cha/c11413.htm), this resolution called on Member States and the Commission, within their respective competencies, to:

- encourage and support the full integration of children and young people with special needs in society through their appropriate education and training, and their insertion in a school system which is adapted to their needs
- make lifelong learning more accessible to people with disabilities and give particular attention to the use of new multimedia technologies and the internet to improve the quality of learning by facilitating access to resources and services as well as remote exchanges and collaboration (e-learning)
- enhance the accessibility of all public websites covering guidance, education and vocational training to persons with disabilities
- increase adequate support of services and technical assistance
- facilitate proper information and guidance
- continue and, if necessary, increase the initial and in-service training of teachers in the area of special needs
- promote European cooperation between the parties involved professionally in the education and training of children and young people with disabilities
- provide facilities, training opportunities and resources regarding the transition from school to employment.

UK legislation and policy

The Special Educational Needs and Disability Act 2001

In 1995, the Disability Discrimination Act (DDA) made it unlawful to discriminate against disabled people in the areas of employment and in the provision of goods and services. In September 2002, the Special Educational Needs and Disability Act 2001 (SENDA) extended the DDA to include education. As a result, all higher and further education institutions and post-16 education providers now have a legal responsibility to students with disabilities.

According to the Code of Practice that relates to the act, educational institutions are expected to be proactive as opposed to reactive when considering and implementing adjustments. The Disability Rights Commission 2002 Code of Practice states that:

> Responsible bodies should not wait until a disabled person applies to a course or tries to use a Service before thinking about what reasonable adjustments they could make. Instead they should continually be anticipating the requirements of disabled people or students and the adjustments they could be making for them, such as regular staff development and reviews of practice. Failure to anticipate the need for an adjustment may mean it is too late to comply with the duty to make the adjustment when it is required. Lack of notice would not of itself provide a defence to an allegation that an adjustment should have been made.

For further information see www.natdisteam.ac.uk/resources_knowledge_SEN_actcovers.html

The Disability Discrimination Act 1995

In 1995 the Disability Discrimination Act (DDA) made it unlawful to discriminate against disabled people in the areas of employment and in the provision of goods and services. The Act uses a wide definition of 'disabled person'. This can include people with:

- physical or mobility impairments
- visual impairments
- hearing impairments
- dyslexia
- medical conditions
- mental health difficulties.

For full details of this act see www.disability.gov.uk/.

The Oxford Student Mental Health Network

A good example of how the disability act has been applied in relation to students within higher and further education is in Oxford where there is specific support information for students with mental health needs at www.brookes.ac.uk/student/services/osmhn.

Known as the Oxford Student Mental Health Network (OSMHN), the project was originally funded for three years up to the end of March 2003 by the Higher Education Funding Council for England (HEFCE). It employed a part-time director, a full-time project manager and a part-time administrator.

The project was a partnership between Oxford Brookes University, the University of Oxford, Oxford College of Further Education, Oxford City Primary Care Trust and Oxfordshire Mental Healthcare NHS Trust.

OSMHN was concerned with research and development, which aimed to:

- promote mental well-being amongst the student population
- support students who develop mental health problems during their studies
- support people with a history of mental health problems who are entering further or higher education.

Much of the materials developed by the OSMHN involved students as participants and consultants. One example of advice on the OSMHN website is on continuing as a student. This states:

> Whilst having a mental health problem can make it difficult to carry on with normal daily life, it is important that students are not put in a position whereby they have to give up on academic life too quickly. Many problems can be resolved, or the effects can be minimised to the point where study can be resumed.

> Some students may need to take time out until they are feeling more in control, others may need to reduce their workload to make things more manageable, whereas some may be able to continue with their studies throughout.

> Whether a student has developed a mental health problem for the first time, or has a previously acquired condition, they should expect: to have access to medical treatment if required; their educational institution to honour its duties to them by making reasonable adjustments in order to take into account the nature of their problems; and not to be discriminated against on the basis of their disability.

The Committee of Vice Chancellors and Principals

In 2000 the Committee of Vice Chancellors and Principals (CVCP), now known as Universities UK, published guidelines on student mental health policies and procedures. These guidelines (CVCP 2000) indicate that educational institutions have certain obligations to students, and state that:

> Care should be taken to ensure that an institution's procedures are not arbitrarily invoked to take inappropriate action against students with mental health difficulties. There is a particular danger, for example, that some students whose mental state causes them to exhibit disturbing behaviour might be inappropriately subject to disciplinary action as a means of exclusion from the institution.

Hull University Project: Responding Effectively to Students' Mental Health Needs

A project carried out by Hull University for HEFCE (Responding Effectively to Students' Mental Health Needs 1996–1999) produced findings that included:

- over one-third of the academic staff respondents from the university have had experience of supervising students with a mental health problem in the previous 5 years
- of these mental health problems, 60% were classified as minor and 28% as 'severe' or 'life threatening'
- the biggest difficulty, faced by 27% of tutors, was getting students to acknowledge their mental health problem and accept help
- 26% of tutors felt they lacked the knowledge, skills and experience needed to deal with students with mental health problems
- 11% of tutors felt they lacked support in their roles from colleagues and other staff members.

The National Service Framework for Mental Health

The National Service Framework for Mental Health (DH 1999) sets out seven key standards for the development of mental health services. Among its recommendations are that health and social services should:

- promote mental health for all, working with individuals and communities
- combat discrimination against individuals and groups with mental health problems, and promote their social inclusion.

For further information about the NSF, see www.dh.gov.uk/mentalhealth.

Valuing People: A Strategy for Learning Disabilities for the 21st Century

Valuing People is a White Paper introduced in 2001. It aims to promote the rights of people with learning disabilities, social inclusion, choice and integration into society. Further information can be found at www.valuingpeople.gov.uk.

International legislation

Higher education institutions in Australia, Canada and the USA have disability policies underpinned by strong equal opportunities and human rights perspectives.

Australia

In Australia the legislation which protect the rights to education and employment of people with disabilities includes The Commonwealth Disability Discrimination Act (1992) and examples of local legislation such as the Queensland Anti-Discrimination Act (1991).

An excellent example of guidance on Working and Studying with a Psychiatric Disability from an Australian University can be found at www.jcu.edu.au/office/disability/psyckit/index.html.

USA

The fundamental principles of non-discrimination and accommodation in academic programmes were set forth in Section 504 of the federal Rehabilitation Act of 1973; the Americans with Disabilities Act of 1990, Title II; and their implementing regulations at 34 C.F.R. Part 104 and 28Ÿ C.F.R. Part 35, respectively.

These laws state that:

> students with disabilities may not, on the basis of their disabilities, be excluded from participation in, be denied the benefits of, or otherwise be subjected to discrimination under any University program or activity. The University must make sure that its academic requirements do not discriminate or have the effect of discriminating against persons with disabilities. Academic requirements that are justifiably essential to a student's program of instruction are not considered discriminatory.

Canada

The Constitution Act (1982), in Canada, includes the Canadian Charter of Rights and Freedoms, which made Canada a leader in establishing the constitutional protection of the equal rights of people with disabilities. All human rights codes in Canada prohibit discrimination on the grounds of 'disability' or 'handicap'.

The 1977 Canadian Human Rights Act (CHRA) is to ensure equality of opportunity without the hindrance or prevention by discrimination in federal jurisdiction. Of specific interest is Section 25 where disability is defined as:

> any previous or existing mental or physical disability and includes disfigurement and previous or existing dependence on alcohol or a drug.

The definition has been interpreted broadly to include perceived disability as well as actual disability. The CHR Tribunal has held that discriminating against someone because of a perception of disability has the same effect as discriminating against someone that is disabled.

Other Canadian acts that relate to disability and discrimination include:

- The Employment Equity Act (EEA) (1995)
- Immigration and Refugee Protection Act (2001)
- The Broadcasting Act (1991).

For further information, see www.hrsdc.gc.ca/asp/gateway.asp?hr=/en/hip/odi/documents/Definitions/Definitions005.shtml&hs= hze.

Glossary and terms

Activity analysis	A way of analysing an activity by breaking it down to see what it requires from the person doing it
Anxiety	A state of worry or apprehension about a possible danger or fear
Assessment	The process of identifying a person's level of knowledge, skill or functional ability
Autism	Any of the group of 'autistic spectrum disorders' characterised by difficulties interacting with others
Bipolar disorder	A mental disorder involving extreme mood swings and sometimes hallucinations
Computer components	See *Hardware*
Depression	A mental disorder characterised by feeling very low in mood for long periods of time, sometimes leading to ideas of self-harm or suicide
Developmental disability	See *Learning disability*
Differentiation	To plan teaching for different levels of ability
Down's syndrome	A type of learning disability resulting from a genetic abnormality characterised by particular physical features and limited cognitive functioning
Functional ability	A person's ability to perform activities
Grading	Breaking down a task into steps to match a person's ability
Hardware	The physical parts of the computer, for example monitor and keyboard
Icon	The pictures on the screen that can be clicked/double-clicked to activate software
Intellectual disability	See *Learning disability*
Learner	The person learning new skills
Learning disability	A significant intellectual impairment with deficits in social functioning and basic everyday skills, which are present from childhood; also known as intellectual disability, developmental disability and mental retardation
Materials	The paperwork and objects used to enhance teaching of new skills
Mental retardation	See *Learning disability*
Occupational therapy	A health profession that focuses on lifestyle rehabilitation through the use of meaningful activities for people with mental or physical disorders or disabilities

Personality disorder | A term used to describe the behaviour associated with the results of psychological trauma or extreme emotional distress

Resources | See *Materials*

Schizophrenia | A mental disorder characterised by positive symptoms, such as hallucinations, and negative symptoms, such as social withdrawal

Session | Any period of time devoted to an activity (or lesson)

Software | The programs used on the computer, for example *Microsoft Word*, *Widgit*, *Out and About*

Stress | Mental or emotional strain or tension

Substance misuse | The inappropriate use of illegal and legal psychoactive drugs (including alcohol and tobacco)

Touch-screen | A screen that allows control of a computer by touching the screen of the monitor

Trackball | A type of computer mouse that involves use of a fixed ball to cause the cursor to move

Selected bibliography

Committee of Vice Chancellors and Principals (CVCP) (2000) *Guidelines on Student Mental Health Policies and Procedures for Higher Education.*

Creek, J. (2001) *Occupational Therapy and Mental Health*, 3rd edition. Edinburgh: Churchill Livingstone.

Davison, G. C. and Neale, J. M. (2000) *Abnormal Psychology*, Wiley International Edition. New York: Wiley.

Department of Health (DH) (1999) *National Service Framework for Mental Health.* London: DH.

Department of Health (2001) *Valuing People: A New Strategy for Learning Disability for the 21st Century.* London: DH.

Department for Education and Employment (DFEE) (2000) *Freedom to Learn: Basic Skills for Learners with Learning Difficulties and/or Disabilities.* Nottingham: DFEE.

Department for Education and Skills (DFES) (2003) *Introducing Access for All: Supporting Learners with Learning Difficulties and Disabilities Across the Curriculum.* Nottingham: DFES Publications.

Department for Education and Skills (DFES) (2002) *Basic Skills for Adults with Learning Difficulties and/or Disabilities: a Resource Pack for Staff.* Nottingham: DFES Publications.

Department for Education and Skills (DFES) (2002) *Self Advocacy Action Pack.* Nottingham: DFES Publications.

Erikson, E. H. and Coles, R. (eds) (2001) *The Erik Erikson Reader.* London: WW Norton & Co.

Further Education Funding Council (FEFC) (1996) *Inclusive Learning Report of the Learning Difficulties and/or Disabilities Committee.* London: FEFC.

Foundation for People with Learning Disabilities (2001) *All About Autistic Spectrum Disorders.* London: Mental Health Foundation.

Napier, R. W. and Gershenfeld, M. K. (1993) *Groups: Theory & Experience*, 5th edition. London: Houghton Mifflin.

Stansfield, J. (ed.) (2001) *A First Handbook of ICT and Special Educational Needs.* Tamworth: National Association for Special Educational Needs (NASEN).

Rogers, A. (2002) *Teaching Adults*, 3rd edition. Maidenhead: Open University Press.

Tomlinson, C. (1999) *The Differentiated Classroom: Responding to the Needs of All Learners.* Alexandria, VA: Association for Supervision and Curriculum Development.

Willis, A. and Orr, S. (2001) *Raising Standards: Initial Assessment of Learning and Support Needs and Planning Learning to Meet Needs.* Nottingham: DFEE Publications.

National Research and Development Centre for Adult Literacy and Numeracy (NRDC), the Institute of Education (IE) and the Basic Skills Agency (BSA) (2003) *Using Laptop Computers to Develop Basic Skills: a Handbook for Practitioners.* London: NRDC Publications.

Index